Examining Mathematics Practice through Classroom Artifacts

Examining Mathematics Practice through Classroom Artifacts

Lynn T. Goldsmith

Nanette M. Seago

Boston   Columbus   Indianapolis   New York   San Francisco   Upper Saddle River
Amsterdam   Cape Town   Dubai   London   Madrid   Milan   Munich   Paris   Montreal   Toronto
Delhi   Mexico City   São Paulo   Sydney   Hong Kong   Seoul   Singapore   Taipei   Tokyo

Vice President, Editor in Chief: Aurora Martínez Ramos
Senior Acquisitions Editor: Kelly Villella Canton
Editorial Assistant: Annalea Manalili
Executive Marketing Manager: Krista Clark
Production Editor: Karen Mason
Production Coordination and Electronic Composition: Element LLC
Text Design and Illustrations: Element LLC
Cover Designer: Jenny Hart
Cover Photo: Candace A. Brooks
Photos: Candace A. Brooks, pp. 1, 31, 64 and Lynn Goldsmith, pp. 7, 14, 48, 61, 72, 85, 89, 104, 114, 120

Videos used on PDToolkit, Video Stills and Transcripts: Copyright © 2011 by San Diego State University Research Foundation. All rights reserved except those explicitly licensed to Pearson Education, Inc. Video was created during IMAP project by Randolph Philipp, Bonnie Schappelle, and Candace Cabral.

Between the time website information is gathered and then published, it is not unusual for some sites to have closed. Also, the transcription of URLs can result in typographical errors. The publisher would appreciate notification where these errors occur so that they may be corrected in subsequent editions.

Library of Congress Cataloging-in-Publication Data

Goldsmith, Lynn T.
    Examining mathematics practice through classroom artifacts / Lynn T. Goldsmith, Nanette Seago.
        p. cm.
    Includes bibliographical references.
    ISBN 978-0-13-210128-8   ISBN 0-13-210128-9
        1. Mathematics—Study and teaching (Middle school)   2. Mathematics—Study and teaching (Primary)   3. Educational evaluation.   4. Curriculum planning.   I. Seago, Nanette.   II. Title.
    QA135.6.G65 2013
    510.71—dc23

                                                                                2011040893

10 9 8 7 6 5 4 3 2 1

PEARSON

ISBN 10:   0-13-210128-9
ISBN 13: 978-0-13-210128-8

About the Authors

Lynn T. Goldsmith

Lynn Goldsmith began her career as a developmental psychologist, where her major research interests lay in understanding the formal and informal systems that support the development of extreme talent. For the past 20 years, she has worked in the field of mathematics education, investigating factors contributing to successful professional development, the role of curriculum in educational reform, and the emotional aspects of learning. She has co-authored *Choosing a Standards-Based Mathematics Curriculum* (Heinemann, 2000), served as series co-editor of the *Guiding Middle-Grades Curriculum Decisions* series (Heinemann, 2000), and co-authored *Nature's Gambit: Child Prodigies and the Development of Human Potential* (Teachers College Press, 1991).

Nanette M. Seago

Nanette Seago was the primary author of *Learning and Teaching Linear Functions: Video Cases for Mathematics Professional Development, 6–12*. She has been working in mathematics professional development for twenty years. Currently, she is working at WestEd as a Principal Investigator for a National Science Foundation project focused on the research and design of videocase materials for middle school teachers—*Learning and Teaching Geometry*.

Contents

Foreword

Is there a difference between *zero* and *nothing*? Or do these two words have the same meaning? It's worth a bit of thought. In fact, you might want to pause right now and think about it for a moment.

Do you have your answer? There are probably many ways in which the words "zero" and "nothing" have different meanings. In fact, given that these two words are about emptiness, it's surprising how full they are of meaning. One way to think about this is that "nothing" is about absence, and it need not be about the absence of anything in particular. "Zero" is at least a little different. When we talk about something having a value of zero, we generally have a particular quantity in mind—we have zero *of something*—which is just a little bit less than having .1 of that same something. That's not quite the same as absence, generally speaking.

One surprising thing about teaching mathematics is how often fine distinctions of this sort matter. In fact, they are often not "fine" distinctions at all. A few weeks ago, I was watching a video clip of an algebra class with a group of high school math teachers. In the video, students are exploring the slopes of horizontal and vertical lines. At one point, a student named Peter suggests correctly that the slope of a horizontal line is zero, explaining that "it's never moving up." A minute or so later, Peter claims, incorrectly, that the slope of a vertical line is also zero. Watching this unfold on the video, we were confused—Peter seemed so confident about the slope of a horizontal line and to really understand why it was zero. Why would he also think the slope of a vertical line is zero? As we talked about this more, Laura, one of the teachers, reflected, "I wonder how many times I just hear 'Zero' and I'm like 'Yup, good job.' Now I wonder what they actually meant. I need to think about this more."

In retrospect, Peter might have been running up against the difference between zero and nothing. A horizontal line has a slope of zero, but a vertical line has no slope. Zero and nothing. Here is a case where this difference really matters. This is not a fine distinction at all. In this case, zero and nothing stand at two opposing poles of a spectrum of possibilities. There is a gaping gulf between them.

Clearly, as teachers, we should be on the lookout for problems of this sort. When we hear a comment from a student or look at a student's written work, we often assume that we understand the thinking behind it. But, like Laura, we might do better to "think about it more." But what does that really mean? What would "thinking about it" entail? How can Laura better "be on the lookout" for the critical nuance in students' thinking? Laura's belief that she needs to think more carefully about what her students understand is a critical step, but on its own, it's likely not enough. What Laura needs is some guidance, some directions for how to productively "think about it." What Laura needs is in this book.

In this volume, Lynn Goldsmith and Nanette Seago offer detailed guidance for "turning to the evidence," for looking closely at classroom artifacts in a deep and substantive manner. The chapters provide a wealth of structure and support for learning to reflect on video and student work in ways that can help teachers productively attend to their students' thinking. So if you're a teacher like Laura, stop reading this foreword and jump ahead! You'll be glad you did, and I'm confident that both you and your students will benefit.

If you're still reading this foreword, then perhaps you have a bit more time to think about how you want to use this book and the messages you'll find. In that case, here are a few suggestions:

- *Engage with an example (and take your time).* One of the richest parts of this volume are the artifacts and the corresponding reflection activities. I found myself immediately drawn in, as I'm sure you will be, when I tried, for example, to understand what Kasage understood about place value (Chapter 2) and how Keisha represented her thinking about perimeter (Chapter 5). At the same time, it was the worksheets that helped to focus my attention on key aspects of the artifacts. As I thought about the mathematics involved in Jose's ideas about lemonade (Chapter 3) and about the cognitive demands in the Fact Families lesson (Chapter 4), I found myself understanding the potential for learning from classroom artifacts in a new way.

- *Notice what and how you notice.* There are some very powerful ideas about noticing in this volume. One issue that the authors discuss in detail in Chapter 2 is the important distinction between describing and interpreting classroom artifacts. As the authors explain, the goal is to develop evidence-based interpretations—ideas about students' thinking based on specifics in the artifacts. Doing so can be challenging, requiring one to step back and first describe the relevant information in the artifact. Learning to identify what appears interesting and important in an artifact, before jumping into an evaluation, is a crucial step in being able to use classroom artifacts as a resource for making sense of students' thinking. A second issue that frames the volume is the need to coordinate attention to students' thinking with attention to mathematics. As the authors make clear, understanding the mathematical entailments of a task is critical background for understanding students' thinking; at the same time, interpreting students' thinking can be revealing about the mathematics involved. To me, a big takeaway from this book is that productively using artifacts to attend to student thinking involves *intentional noticing*. It involves being aware of whether you are describing or interpreting, focusing on issues of thinking or of content, and being aware of how these different aspects of noticing play a role in making sense of students' thinking. As the author themselves explain,

> "Looking" at student work or at video involves more than just *looking*. It involves knowing what to look *for*, how to interpret what you see, and how to use your interpretations to plan (and undertake) instructional moves that will push student thinking forward." (p. xvi)

- *Make these practices your own.* If all you do is read this book and go through the exercises, you'll probably develop an appreciation for analyzing classroom artifacts and the sense that student work and video really are gold mines for learning about students' thinking. But until you make these practices your own and try them with *your* students in *your* classroom, you won't fully experience the benefit of the ideas introduced here. Throughout the volume, the authors offer practical advice for taking these ideas back to your classroom—exploring different representations in a warm-up activity, sorting a set of homework papers, conducting interviews with individual students, and more. In deciding how to proceed, you'll want to consider where in the life of your classroom you typically find windows into student thinking. And don't restrict yourself to the suggestions from the authors; part of the fun will be expanding beyond the recommendations in the book.

The use of classroom artifacts to ground teacher learning has become quite popular in teacher education and professional development today—and with good reason. Such artifacts provide an important bridge between learning that happens outside the classroom and the skills and knowledge that teachers apply within the classroom. In the moment of instruction, it can be quite difficult to make sense of students' comments or methods. Investigating classroom artifacts using the techniques introduced here will help teachers become familiar with productive ways to explore students' mathematical thinking. This book will both inspire teachers to want to make sense of their students' thinking and provide them with the tools to do so.

Miriam Gamoran Sherin
Associate Professor, School of Education
and Social Policy
Northwestern University
August, 2011

Preface

This book grew out of our Turning to the Evidence (TTE) project, which we began in 2002 with our colleagues Mark Driscoll and Judy Mumme with support from the National Science Foundation. The motivation for the project came from our desire to know more about how professional development worked when it centered around exploration of "classroom artifacts"—physical records that capture aspects of the work that happens during mathematics lessons such as video of classroom discussions, samples of students' written work, and transcripts of students' small-group problem solving.

"Looking at student work" has, in fact, become such a popular element of professional development that there are a number of books and Web pages devoted to work with this particular kind of classroom artifact (see, e.g., Allen & Blythe, 2004; Blythe, Allen, & Powell, 1999; websites such as http://www.lasw.org and http://www. middleweb.com/LASW). In fact, in June 2011, searching the phrase "looking at student work" yielded close to 22,000,000 hits! With the advent of smaller and less expensive video recording equipment, "looking at video" is joining "looking at student work" as a popular vehicle for teachers' professional development (Borko, Jacobs, Eiteljorg, & Pittman, 2008; Seago, 2004; Sherin, 2004; van Es & Sherin, 2008).

Yet Nanette, Mark, and Judy knew from their many years of experience that it requires a great deal of thought, planning, and skillful facilitation to use artifacts like video and written student work productively in professional development settings. We also knew from our work in districts and schools and our participation in professional organizations that many people using artifacts in professional development contexts lacked clear, principled strategies for using them to explore critical issues of learning and teaching. We began to see similarities between the ways professional development has embraced the use of artifacts for promoting teachers' learning and the ways manipulatives have been touted for classroom use. Nearly 20 years ago, Deborah Ball described the "magical hopes" that many educators seemed to have invested in manipulatives:

> My main concern about the enormous faith in the power of manipulatives, in their almost magical ability to enlighten, is that we will be misled into thinking that mathematical knowledge will automatically rise from their use. Would that it were so! Unfortunately, creating effective vehicles

for learning mathematics requires more than just a catalog of promising manipulatives. The context in which any vehicle—concrete or pictorial—is used is as important as the material itself. By context, I mean the ways in which students work with the materials, toward what purposes, with what kind of talk and instruction. . . . The manipulative itself cannot on its own carry the intended [mathematical] meanings and uses. (Ball, 1992, p. 18)

If you substitute "classroom artifacts" for "manipulatives" in this quote and change the context from the classroom to professional development, then Ball would have eloquently captured the optimistic belief that using classroom artifacts will automatically enlighten teachers about their mathematics instruction. This just isn't the case. Like manipulatives, classroom artifacts are *tools*—and like most tools, they're effective only when used skillfully and appropriately. "Looking" at student work or at video involves more than just *looking*. It involves knowing what to look *for*, how to interpret what you see, and how to use your interpretations to plan (and undertake) instructional moves that will push students' thinking forward.

During the TTE project (and beyond), we've worked to help teachers develop the skills and dispositions to use classroom artifacts to investigate mathematics learning and teaching. As part of our effort to dispel potential magical hopes associated with artifacts, we've developed the Skillful Use of Artifacts framework to help guide artifact-based inquiry (Nikula, Goldsmith, Blasi, & Seago, 2006). The framework emphasizes that skillful work with artifacts requires attention to both the mathematical thinking and the mathematical content embodied in artifacts (see below). Attention to only one or the other isn't enough since our job as teachers is to gauge students' thinking and to plan instructional courses of action to promote their understanding of concepts and acquisition of the skills and habits of mind for a defined body of mathematical knowledge. We need to analyze students' thinking in the context of target mathematical ideas and processes. This framework, which we introduce in Chapter 1, helps organize the book.

Skillful Use of Artifacts

SKILLFUL USE OF ARTIFACTS INVOLVES:

Attention to Thinking	Attention to Content
▶ distinguish between description and interpretation of work represented in artifacts	▶ use a guiding mathematical framework to discuss the mathematical content in artifacts
▶ ground interpretations of thinking in evidence from artifacts	▶ compare/contrast different representations of mathematical ideas captured in artifacts
▶ generate plausible alternative interpretations of thinking and justify ideas with evidence	▶ compare/contrast mathematical explanations and solution methods represented in artifacts
▶ see strengths (not just weaknesses) in thinking and understanding captured in artifacts	▶ use the exploration of mathematics to develop/ engage norms of mathematical argument

Source: Adapted from Nikula, J., Goldsmith, L. T., Blasi, Z. V., & Seago, N. (2006). A framework for the strategic use of classroom artifacts in mathematics professional development. *NCSM Journal, 9*(1), 59.

We've designed this book to provide guidance and practice in using a variety of artifacts in the hope that you will learn to make effective use of your own classroom artifacts as well as ones you might encounter in professional development settings in the future. The chapters are organized around various aspects of the Skillful Use of Artifacts framework and are designed to provide opportunities for you to refine your eye for attending to and interpreting students' mathematical thinking. We've also sought to make connections to important mathematical ideas and practices. Where applicable, each chapter includes marginal boxes referencing the Common Core State Standards content and practices (Common Core State Standards, 2010).

Chapter 1 introduces you to our perspective on investigating mathematics teaching and learning and to the framework for using artifacts skillfully. The remainder of the book is divided into three sections, each of which explores the Skillful Use of Artifacts framework from a different vantage point. Section 1 takes a close look at the left-hand column of the framework, focusing on using artifacts to inquire into students' thinking. In Chapter 2, we distinguish between *describing* students' work and using those descriptions to posit and explore plausible *interpretations* of their thinking. We emphasize the importance of suspending judgment and approaching artifacts with a stance of curious inquiry—what can we learn about the mathematics, students' thinking, and possibly teachers' instructional decisions rather than how we might fix what we see is problematic in either students or teachers. We work with three different kinds of artifacts in Chapter 2: a written description of a student as he works on a task, videotaped interviews of individual students working on math problems, and a set of students' solutions to a problem posed in class. Chapter 3 uses video clips of class discussions to investigate students' mathematical errors and explore ways that errors might be embraced rather than avoided in class.

Section 2 addresses the right-hand column of the framework, focusing attention on mathematical content. In Chapter 4, we work with your own textbook and some sample lessons as we consider the importance of having a clear sense of the important mathematics driving the math curriculum. Chapter 5 uses written descriptions of classroom work and video of classroom discussions to explore how different representations can convey a mathematical concept in somewhat different ways. We'll also use Chapter 5 to consider the importance of understanding the variety of ways students think about and represent mathematical situations.

The third section of the book offers the chance for you to take a broader and more integrative perspective. Chapter 6 brings our work in the first two sections together, combining attention to content and to student thinking and integrating the individual pieces we've explored in the previous chapters. In this chapter, we investigate how a lesson unfolds over an entire class period.

Features of This Book

In each of the first five chapters, we intentionally focus in on small slices of classroom life to give you the opportunity to practice potentially new ways of seeing and thinking. We want to provide the opportunity to consider individual elements of a complex practice without becoming overwhelmed, even though we recognize that, by guiding your focus in a particular direction, we are (at least temporarily) ignoring other important aspects of classroom life.

Chapters 2 to 6 include sample artifacts, practice exercises, and worksheets. The chapters provide step-by-step suggestions for working through the exercises, study questions, and short commentaries to help promote reflection and discussion in professional learning communities, book study groups, workshops, and other professional development settings. We also encourage you to use the worksheets (as is or with modifications) to explore artifacts from your own classes. In fact, although we developed the Skillful Use of Artifacts framework in the context of mathematics, we think that the processes it describes are applicable to instruction in other subjects too and, with appropriate modifications, could be useful for thinking about teaching science, social studies, or language arts. After all, the emphasis on attention to both content and thinking are important to learning and teaching any content domain, as the Common Core State Standards attest.

Throughout the book, therefore, it's important that you acquaint yourself with the mathematical aspects of artifacts, even when our primary focus is on attending to students' thinking. You'll notice that each exercise begins with a request for you to either work the problem used in the artifact or, at the very least, think about the mathematical ideas on which it's based. We also want to urge you to take a respectful and nonevaluative attitude toward those students and teachers who have agreed to make their work public. As we discuss in Chapter 1, people naturally label and categorize—and often judge as well—but not always for the better. Our purpose in this book is to focus on artifacts to develop the skills—and the dispositions to use them—that will provide insights about learning and teaching, not to focus on speculations about what individual learners or teachers could or even should have done in a particular instance.

Ways to Use This Book

We've structured the book to be flexible and responsive to individual needs. Chapter 2 ("Describing and Interpreting Classroom Artifacts") lays out an important distinction between describing the evidence of student thinking available in artifacts from interpreting that evidence and provides a conceptual basis for the work that follows. For this reason, we suggest that you read this chapter before subsequent chapters. We've organized the remaining sections and chapters into a sequence that we think offers an orderly progression but recognize that there might be another order that seems more relevant or interesting to you and your own needs.

For example, we encountered a chicken-and-egg dilemma in ordering the sections on attending to thinking and attending to mathematical content. *Both* of these foci are equally critical to using artifacts skillfully, but the hard-copy book format requires us to consider them sequentially. We've chosen to begin with a section on student thinking because ultimately it's students' ideas that we seek to shape and grow yet we also fully acknowledge that Section 2 is critical to the whole story since we are shaping and growing those ideas toward a set of agreed-on mathematical knowledge, skills, and practices (see Common Core Standards, 2010; National Council of Teachers of Mathematics, 1989, 2000). Therefore, if you would prefer to take a different path through the chapters in the book, by all means give it a try.

We have also envisioned this book being used in different ways—as a resource you are exploring independently, as something you are discussing with a colleague, or as part of a teacher study group. We have tried to make the book useful to people working in any of these configurations by offering commentaries on some of the student work. Our own vision for the book was that it would be part of some collaborative venture. Learning is rarely a solitary activity; there's much to be gained, both intellectually and in terms of motivation and support, by working with others. When people work together, they offer each other different perspectives and experiences that invariably enrich the conversation and raise issues to debate and explore. To this end, we've included a book study guide at the end of the book to support teachers who may want to work through this book together.

Because we've written this book for teachers in elementary and middle school, we've chosen math examples from a range of grade levels. You may therefore feel a closer connection to some of the exercises than others. We think that there's value, however, in considering problems that are typically part of the curriculum of students who are either younger or older than your own. When you work across the grade span, you can develop a deeper appreciation for how mathematical ideas (as well as mathematics programs) articulate—what are the ideas and skills that students need to have in place before they get to you, and how will your year with them help prepare them for the ideas and skills they will encounter as they move on in school? We hope that you will also come to appreciate the interesting mathematical ideas that even very young children grapple with and to discover that younger students often have resources for thinking about problems that are "billed" as belonging to upper elementary or middle school years.

Our goal throughout this book is to support you in learning about and trying out various ways to use classroom artifacts to enrich your practice and, ultimately, your students' learning. We hope that you find the book interesting and useful.

PDToolkit for *Examining Mathematics Practice through Classroom Artifacts*

PDToolkit
for
Examining Mathematics Practice through Classroom Artifacts

Accompanying this book there is a website with media resources that, together with the text, provide you the tools you need to fully explore and implement the concepts presented here. The PDToolkit for *Examining Mathematics Practice through Classroom Artifacts* is available free for six months after you register using the access code that comes with this book. After that, it is available by subscription for a yearly fee. Be sure to explore and download the resources available at the website. The following resources will be available:

- Video clips referenced throughout this text
- Downloadable Worksheets from this book (the asterisk next to the Worksheet title on page 135 indicates which are writable)

CourseSmart eBook and other eBook Options Available

CourseSmart is an exciting new choice for purchasing this book. As an alternative to purchasing the printed book, you may purchase an electronic version of the same content via CourseSmart for reading on PC, Mac, as well as Android devices, iPad, iPhone, and iPod Touch with CourseSmart Apps. With a CourseSmart eBook, readers can search the text, make notes online, and bookmark important passages for later review. For more information or to purchase access to the CourseSmart eBook, visit http://www.coursesmart.com. Also look for availability of this book on a number of other eBook devices and platforms.

Acknowledgments

We've had the good fortune to work with a number of generous and thoughtful colleagues who have helped to shape our thinking and continue to make our work fun. Mark Driscoll and Judy Mumme were there at the very beginning of the original Turning to the Evidence project, helping to design the work and generously offering their wealth of experience as seasoned professional developers and professional development providers. Mark worked with us throughout the project as seminar facilitator and collaborator. He also made sure that the overall level of levity and comic irony remained consistently high. Johannah Nikula and Zuzka Blasi ably rounded out the project staff and were always game for taking on new challenges; Dan Heck served as our external evaluator and statistician supreme. Many thanks also go to all the teachers who participated in TTE and in subsequent professional development that we've either facilitated or observed—it's the chance to join teachers in their efforts to better serve their students that makes our work possible. We'd also like to thank Jim Dietz and Elizabeth VanderPutten for their interest and engagement with our work before, during, and after the project itself, and to the National Science Foundation for supporting the TTE project under grant REC-0231892 (although the work in this book does not necessarily reflect the views of the foundation itself).

We also want to thank those colleagues who have provided lively and fascinating conversations over the years with respect to both the TTE project specifically and, more generally, mathematics education (and assorted other topics). Thanks to Deborah Ball, Hilda Borko, Patrick Callahan, Cathy Carroll, Helen Doerr, Megan Franke, Paul Goldenberg, Jennifer Jacobs, Vicki Jacobs, Catherine Lewis, Raven McCrory, June Mark, Amy Morse, Barbara Scott Nelson, Randy Philipp, Arthur Powell, Kristen Reed, Deborah Schifter, Miriam Sherin, Marty Simon, Beth van Es, and Judi Zawojewski for helping us develop and refine our thinking. Thanks too to Ilene Kantrov, who has always been at the ready with time to listen to nascent ideas and to apply that "friendly" red pencil to drafts in progress.

Kelly Villella Canton, Senior Acquisitions Editor, has supported the development of this book at every point along the way, providing the wise counsel needed to shape an originally academic endeavor into a product intended for a wider audience. Her incisive observations, always delivered with cheerful encouragement, have been of enormous help. Julia Hendrix provided feedback on several chapters from her perspective as mathematics specialist, and she and "her" teachers generously invited us into a number of classrooms for visits. Karen Mason, Annalea Manalili, Barbara Hawk, and Bruce Owens have helped to shepherd the manuscript into a "real" book with skill and humor.

The reviewers who commented on the book proposal, chapters, or manuscript drafts at Pearson's request also contributed insights that shaped the final product. We thank the following reviewers: Victoria Bohidar, Hopkins Road Elementary School; Stephen Currie, Poughkeepsie Day School; Julie A. Drewry, Roanoke City Public Schools; Linda S. Gater, Jackson Public Schools; Jane Elizabeth Gillis; Red Clay Consolidated School District; Deborah Gordon, Madison Simis School; Michelle J. Guy, Jackson Public School District; Carrie Hall Zielinski, Oakland Schools; Margaret Heritage, National Center for Research on Evaluation, Standards and Student Testing (CRESST) at University of California, Los Angeles; Denise Justice, Raceland Worthington Independent School District; Ruth Ann Kinker, South Hill Elementary; Helen J. Mathews, Mary Calcott Elementary School; Karen Roberts, Montgomery County Public Schools; Dori B. Walk, Staunton City Schools; Rebecca Walter, Ghent School; and Tisha Wilson Hyman, Oakwood Elementary School.

Our families encouraged us to take on the challenge of writing this book, marshalling the support and culinary/takeout skills needed when a spouse/mom says, "It'll just take a minute while I get this sentence right" and then finally pushes away from the computer two hours later. Thanks for hanging in there with us.

Turning to the Evidence

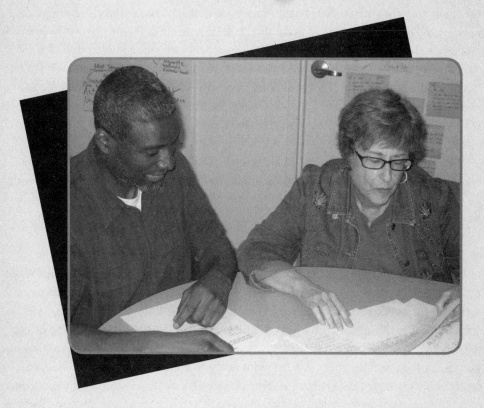

Jeffrey Stockdale starts his fifth-grade math lesson with homework review. He turns to the homework assignment in the teacher's edition of his textbook and looks out at his class, seated in table groups of four and six. "Your homework was about adding and subtracting fractions. Get out your papers and trade with your table partner so we can check answers." Students find their homework and make their trades; Jeffrey calls on Emma for the answer to the first problem. "Jon's paper says $\frac{1}{3}$ of a dozen eggs." She glances over at her own paper, which Jon is checking. "That's what I got, too." Jeffrey confirms that $\frac{1}{3}$ dozen is the correct answer, scanning the room quickly to see if all the students seem to be with him. Students mark their papers and wait patiently for the next problem. He continues through the rest of the homework, calling on different students to supply answers and working through solutions if there are any questions. When they finish, Jeffrey instructs his students to write the number of problems correctly solved at the top of the page. He collects all the papers and moves on to the day's lesson. After school, he'll note the homework scores in his grade book and put the papers in the Homework Return bin. They'll stay there until the end of the day on Friday, when he'll toss any unclaimed papers as he straightens his room for the weekend.

Jeffrey Stockdale is sitting on a potential gold mine, but he doesn't know it—his students' homework papers are an untapped resource for his math teaching. Jeffrey assigns homework so that students can practice using the math they've just studied in class, and he checks papers to make sure that the kids are doing their work. Homework grades also help him keep an eye out for those students who aren't doing well. Jeffrey clearly recognizes the value of homework as a flag for students' *performance*. What he hasn't yet thought about is homework (and other information from his classroom) as a window into his students' *thinking*—a window that could help him to better diagnose what his students do and don't understand and therefore help to guide his instructional plans.

Jeffrey can open that window by thinking differently about what homework tells him about his students. Class discussion, homework, in-class group work, and tests can all reveal a lot more about how his students are thinking than simply whether they solved a problem correctly. He already recognizes this to some degree since he regularly gives students partial credit for their work; he can further boost his insights into students' understanding by learning to view his students' work in new ways. At present, he basically has a single lens that focuses on the correctness of students' answers. When many students make substantive (rather than "careless") errors, he knows he has to review or reteach; when most students' work is correct, he knows he can move on to something new. But Jeffrey can get more mileage out of his students' work if he brings in other lenses as well. A *mathematics* lens will help him think about the mathematical purpose of the assignment and can help him assess students' work more precisely in terms of his mathematical goals. A *student thinking* lens will help him look for evidence of *how* his students understand the math and can help him get a clearer picture of where they're on target and where they're not. If Jeffrey uses multiple lenses instead of just his *are they right?* one, he gains more information about his students—information that can help guide his instruction. He will know more about the strengths and weaknesses in his students' mathematical understanding, and he'll be able to pinpoint more accurately the kinds of upcoming mathematical tasks and conversations that will promote solid learning.

In this book, we aim to support you in taking advantage of your own gold mine by developing lenses that will focus you more sharply on students' mathematical understanding and reasoning. The better handle you can get on students' thinking, the better you'll be positioned to make judicious instructional decisions that will help move their understanding forward. We'll work on developing those lenses by working with different kinds of artifacts from math classrooms—samples of students' work, video and/or transcripts of math discussions in class, and lessons from your textbook—to develop and refine your ability to analyze student thinking, connect students' ideas to important mathematical concepts, and apply these analyses to the daily work of planning and carrying out lessons.

What Are Artifacts, and Why Analyze Them?

Broadly speaking, artifacts are objects that people make. You probably think about them in the context of archaeology, where material remains like pottery sherds, systems of cisterns and water pipes, ruins of buildings, and even the contents of old garbage dumps help us create accounts of earlier lives and times. But artifacts aren't only broken or buried remnants of times gone by. Your own classroom is full of them. Completed math assignments, cast-off scratch papers, and problem solutions that students share on the board or overhead are all examples of artifacts from math class. So, too, are the lessons from your textbook, the work you present on the board or overhead as you introduce an activity or work through a problem solution, and the comments you write on student papers. Audio- and videotaped records of lessons are becoming increasingly popular classroom artifacts. All these examples are potentially rich with information that can help you be more tuned into your students' mathematical understanding.

So how are artifacts useful for improving your practice? As we noted in the vignette about Jeffrey Stockdale, artifacts can serve as windows into students' thinking, and it's the development of students' thinking that is at the core of our work as teachers. If we are to help shape what students know by building on their current ideas and skills, we need to sort out what aspects of their thinking are irrelevant or incorrect and what aspects are absent, nascent, or incomplete. By listening to students and examining their work, we can gain insights into the nature of their understanding and plan learning opportunities accordingly.

Artifacts are also useful for learning to zero in on what's important in math class. As a teacher, you're called on to make hundreds of on-the-fly decisions over the course of a day. Some of these decisions are about where you should be focusing your attention, some are about what you will attend to, and some are about how you'll respond to what you're noticing (Jacobs, Lamb, & Philipp, 2010). Classroom life itself is so fast paced that you are often making these decisions without even being aware of how you're processing information. As you scan the room, for example, you know that Cecelia and Libby are goofing off in the far left-hand corner of the room just as sure as you know that Justin and Jennifer are on task, even though both pairs of students are talking animatedly and laying out base-10 blocks, and you would be hard pressed to say, right then and there, exactly how you can tell the difference. Working with artifacts offers the opportunity to explore classroom events and student work without the real-time pressure of having to register, interpret, and respond to them as they are actually occurring. Examining artifacts *from* the classroom but *outside* of the classroom allows for more leisurely analysis, discussion, and reflection on issues related to mathematics, mathematics learning, and mathematics teaching. Investigating classroom artifacts can help you develop and practice new ways of noticing and interpreting students' thinking, imagining questions you might ask to gather more information about their ideas, and planning lessons and activities.

By learning how to use multiple lenses to analyze classroom artifacts, you'll be developing more tools to help you focus your teaching on your students' strengths as well as to their learning needs. In this book we'll focus on developing the following:

- Specific ways to examine and analyze students' mathematical thinking
- Skills at honing in on specific mathematics that can emerge in student interactions and presentations
- Increased awareness of possible student reasoning that lies beneath both correct and incorrect answers

Learning to See through Multiple Lenses

To work with classroom artifacts productively, we need to know how to attend to information they contain. It turns out that the way we attend to information involves an interesting mix of perceiving and interpreting those perceptions—what we know drives what we can see, and what we see drives what we can know and learn.

We all make thousands of decisions every day about where to pay attention and what to ignore. Virtually every task you undertake requires you to notice some aspects of the environment and to ignore others. When you're driving down the street, chances are that you don't notice the colors of the clothes that people on the sidewalk are wearing (you may not even notice the people themselves). If you decide to give yourself a treat and go to a coffee shop to finish the fabulous thriller you're reading, you probably don't register the comings and goings of other patrons.

Psychologists Daniel Simons, Chris Chabris, and their colleagues have studied how people filter what they attend to in a provocative series of studies about processing unexpected events. In one study, participants watched a video of two basketball teams. Each team of three players passes a ball among their teammates. Study participants were instructed to count the number of passes made by one of the teams. About half-way through the video, an unexpected event occurred. Some participants saw a woman carrying an umbrella walk right through the middle of the game. Others saw a version of the video where a person in a gorilla costume ambled through the game, stopping briefly in the middle of the frame to look at the camera and perform the prototypical gorilla "chest pound" before completing the stroll through the scene. Overall, nearly half the participants failed to notice the anomalous event at all. The study dramatically illustrates that focusing intently on a task can "blind" you to other, seemingly attention-grabbing aspects of your environment. (Try this basketball task—and others—with an unsuspecting friend. You can read about the study in *The Invisible Gorilla* [Chabris & Simons, 2010] and find videos at http://www.theinvisiblegorilla.com and http://www.youtube.com/user/profsimons.)

Now, we don't mean to suggest that you would miss Mary Poppins or King Kong ambling through your classroom, even if you *were* attending closely to something your students were saying or doing. But we do want to emphasize that it's impossible to monitor everything that's happening in a room with 20 or 30 (or maybe even more) students in it. In fact, it's imperative that we tune out some information in order to focus on the events that are really important.

Our attention isn't influenced only by competing demands—expectations can also narrow what we attend to and therefore the information that we process, even when we're not preoccupied with other tasks. For example, previous experiences with our students can lead us to anticipate their level of success and the amount of additional support they may need in completing tasks. But our expectations themselves may obscure students' strengths or weaknesses.

Take the case of Ms. Hamlin and Cindy. We observed Ms. Hamlin's seventh-grade class as they were beginning a geometry unit. The lesson involved using pentominoes to create congruent figures. It was springtime, and teacher and students knew each other quite well by this time of the year. Ms. Hamlin asked her students to make four or five congruent figures from the pentominoes. Because she felt the activity was a challenging one, she debated whether she should use a simpler, potentially less frustrating activity with her weaker students but decided to give the lesson a try "as is" with the whole group. One of the students she was concerned about was Cindy, a quiet girl on an individualized education plan who struggled with basic math facts and consistently needed extra math support in and out of class. Cindy found 20 congruent figures almost before Ms. Hamlin had finished passing out the materials. Ms. Hamlin was bowled over by Cindy's ability to think spatially. She was equally surprised by the difficulties she saw among some of her "gifted and talented" students and was puzzled about where they were getting tripped up.

In this instance, Ms. Hamlin decided to override her expectation that the lesson would be too difficult for her less able students. What if she'd gone with her concerns and had presented an alternative, "dumbed-down" lesson for students like Cindy—or if she'd decided not to use the lesson at all but to substitute a much simpler one? Had she made either of these decisions, she wouldn't have discovered that Cindy had powerful ways of thinking spatially—ways that the more traditionally talented math students seemed to lack. She also wouldn't have seen the pride and confidence that Cindy displayed during that lesson or the respect shown her by the other students. Hopefully, Ms. Hamlin began to look for other instances of Cindy's mathematical strengths and to explore ways to use her strong spatial reasoning to help her understand other math ideas.

Our Vision of Mathematics Learning and Teaching

Our vision of mathematics learning and teaching corresponds closely to that articulated by the National Council of Teachers of Mathematics (NCTM, 2000, 2006) and, more recently, the Common Core State Standards (CCSS, 2010). Central to this vision is the notion that we all actively build knowledge and understanding through our efforts to make sense of our experiences. We interpret new experiences—a demonstration in class, a discussion with a friend, or the unexpected results of an event or activity—in terms of what we currently know and we also stretch our existing understanding to accommodate our new encounters (Lave, 1988; Lave & Wenger, 1991; Piaget, 1970; Werner, 1948; Wertsch, 1985). None of our learning begins with a totally blank slate or with simply adopting ideas wholesale from the outside. Instead, learning proceeds by using what we already know to make sense of our new experiences with people, objects, and ideas, gradually shaping our understanding into more complete, complex, and interconnected knowledge.

This view of learning has implications for instruction. For example, effective teaching explicitly engages students in sense making by having students explain and justify their reasoning. It also emphasizes work that's "authentic"—meaningful, valuable, and representative of the kinds of activities and thinking that engage actual practitioners of the discipline instead of just rote make-work. For math teaching, this means helping students learn to *do* mathematics—to learn to think and inquire with the same kinds of tools and approaches that practicing mathematicians use. This goal is what's behind the process principles articulated in NCTM documents and, more recently, in the CCSS Mathematical Practices (see Table 1.1).

TABLE 1.1 Common Core State Standards for Mathematical Practice

MATHEMATICAL PRACTICES
1. Make sense of problems and persevere in solving them.
2. Reasons abstractly and quantitatively.
3. Construct viable arguments and critique the reasoning of others.
4. Model with mathematics.
5. Use appropriate tools strategically.
6. Attend to precision.
7. Look for and make use of structure.
8. Look for and express regularity in repeated reasoning.

Source: Copyright © 2010. National Governors Association Center for Best Practices and Council of Chief State School Officers. All rights reserved.

This view of learning as an active, constructive process and the emphasis on sense making means that each student will understand the work you do in class in his or her own way. This view is sometimes challenging to keep in mind with respect to students' mathematical work. It's fairly common for people to assume that others approach math problems pretty much the same way they do; for those of us who were taught that the way to solve problems was the way the teacher showed us, this tendency might be even stronger. But even when math was about memorizing facts and procedures, we weren't necessarily all thinking exactly the way the teacher taught us. We know a man in his late 50s who remembers being taught that the "right" way to add long columns of numbers was to start at the top of the column and muscle your way straight down to the bottom. Although he knew his math facts and could have worked from top to bottom, when faced with long columns of numbers to add, he would try to simplify his task by secretly finding pairs of digits in the column that summed to 10. He also firmly believed that he was cheating by looking for the easy combinations. Today, he would be applauded for his number sense. At the time, he believed that he would have been chided for his lack of raw computational power if his teacher had known how he was solving the problems.

It's therefore important to keep in mind that we can't always assume we know how students are thinking from just having the final products of their work. Sometimes students can get correct answers despite tangled thinking. Conversely, students who produce incorrect answers can still have used promising and productive approaches. One of the big challenges we face as teachers is figuring out whether students' *reasoning* is sound, not just whether their *answers* are right or wrong.

This student's partner used four cubes to build a train representing a value of 20; the teacher asks, "in your train, how much is a cube worth?"

After more than 20 years of mathematics education reform, most teachers are open to the idea that learning mathematics involves developing conceptual understanding as well as gaining computational skill and accuracy. They're also open to the idea that not all students think about the mathematics they are learning in exactly the same way. This view fits much better with psychological theory and research about learning, but it also places a bigger burden on you, as the teacher, to better understand your students' thinking and to remember that you can't assume that students will easily grasp ideas that seem to you to be simple and perhaps even obvious.

Take as an example the nearly ubiquitous use of base-10 blocks to teach about place value. Because seeing the "ten-ness" in these materials is quite straightforward to us, it's difficult to imagine that this wouldn't be the case for children as well. But remember, we already understand our number system, so the unit cubes, rods, flats, and large (1000s) cubes offer us a straightforward way to represent an already well-developed set of ideas about powers of 10 and ways that we write numbers to represent the values of different "places."

But consider Zach, a second grader we observed during a lesson in which students were using base-10 blocks to solve addition problems using regrouping. He seemed to be having a lot of trouble remembering to trade 10 unit cubes for a rod when representing his answer. As he worked, we realized that his difficulty was not simply a matter of forgetting to make the trades. Despite his teacher's repeated reminders that he needed to trade 10 unit cubes for a rod, he didn't really understand that the rod represented a group of 10 units.

On three separate occasions, his teacher Betsy came over to him to work one-on-one, and each time Betsy asked him how many unit cubes were "in" the rod. This was not a trivial or obvious question to him—each time she asked, he had to check. The first time, Zach put the rod on the floor and lined up unit cubes next to it. Because the nubby carpet and his own motor limitations made this task difficult, he couldn't align them without leaving some space between the cubes, and he could fit only eight in a row alongside of the rod (see Figure 1.1). He looked up at her and answered, somewhat hesitantly, "eight?"

Betsy responded by suggesting that he put the unit cubes on top of the rod instead of beside it. Doing it this way, Zach aligned the 10 unit cubes along the rod, counted, and

Figure 1.1   Zach's base-10 block arrangement

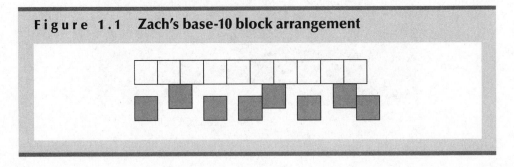

said that there were 10 units in the rod. To confirm his work, she took off the unit blocks, held up the rod, and pointed to each segment as he counted each of the 10 segments. Three or four minutes later, she came back over and asked him again how many blocks were in the rod. Again he had to count. This time he miscounted and answered, "nine." He seemed unperturbed when Betsy reminded him that they'd counted the rod and gotten 10 blocks a few minutes before. They reestablished that there were 10 blocks in the rod, but a few minutes later, Zach was once again unsure.

Adults know in their bones that the rod represents 10 unit cubes and that this quantity is stable. Many second graders see the situation similarly, but some are still developing this understanding. Zach seemed to still be in this "under development" phase. His lack of certainty about the number of unit cubes that made up a rod and his comfort with assigning a different value to the rod each time he counted its segments suggests that he had yet to firmly establish a one-to-one correspondence between the number of segments in the rod and the count of those segments. Until he understands this relationship, he will see something different in the base-10 blocks than his teacher Betsy does. And until he does, the rod will not help him understand the idea of bundling units into groups of 10 during addition or subtraction.

It's likely that at least some of your students, too, will wrestle with ideas in math class that you have assumed would be simple and straightforward to them. Sometimes figuring out what, exactly, is the source of the problem can be challenging and time consuming. Sometimes, the challenge is to decide whether a student's different way of thinking is sensible and valid. Other times, your challenge involves thinking about how to address students' errors in a way that will help them better understand the math.

For example, it's not uncommon for teachers to chalk up multidigit addition errors to students' carelessness in forgetting to "carry" when writing their answers. Here are two examples of incorrect problem solutions that might be interpreted this way (see Figure 1.2). But let's stop and consider these errors a moment. How would you interpret them? Do they seem similar to you? Why (or why not)?

To us, they appear quite different. We could imagine that Ethan might, in fact, have simply forgotten to record his regrouping (and "carry" the extra 10) when he added $5 + 7$. Nothing about Asheran's answer, though, looks like an oversight or a careless error to us. Instead, we think there's something either about the structure of our number system itself or about the way that we write numbers using place value that she's still trying to figure out. While Ethan's teacher may need do no more than ask him whether he's satisfied with his answer or to tell him he's made a computational error he should look for, Asheran's teacher will likely want to spend some time with her trying to understand what it is that she does and doesn't yet understand.

Our point here is that recent theory and research emphasize that we can't assume that others think about mathematics exactly the same way we do—particularly when those others are children. Our vision of mathematics teaching includes cultivating the

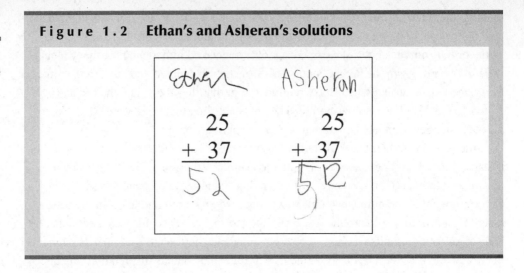

Figure 1.2   Ethan's and Asheran's solutions

disposition to attend to the details of students' thinking, recognizing novel as well as common approaches to problems, assessing the mathematical validity of students' work, and helping students draw connections between their thinking and important mathematical ideas and skills.

A Framework for Using Artifacts Skillfully

So how can you cultivate these approaches to teaching? We think that a promising approach is to tap into that potential gold mine that classroom artifacts offer to inquire into students' mathematical thinking. But tapping the mother lode involves knowing how to release the gold; prospecting for information about students' thinking with artifacts is surely more effective when you know where and what to look for. We developed the Skillful Use of Artifacts framework, described briefly in this book's preface, to help you focus your efforts where the payoff is likely to be worthwhile.

The framework highlights the importance of attending to both the mathematical thinking and the mathematical content embodied in the artifact. It also articulates specific strategies for engaging with artifacts in the service of these two main foci of attention. You can think about these strategies as tools for polishing those new lenses you're using to understand the mathematical work you and your students undertake in class.

For example, the entries in the "Attention to Thinking" column of Table 1.1 offer strategies to help you get a clearer idea of how students make sense of the mathematics they are working on. Instead of *assuming* that you understand what students are thinking, these strategies help you set your own perspective aside and use classroom artifacts as data to examine for evidence of how—and possibly why—students approached problems

TABLE 1.2 Skillful Use of Artifacts	
SKILLFUL USE OF ARTIFACTS INVOLVES:	
Attention to Thinking	**Attention to Content**
▶ distinguish between description and interpretation of work represented in artifacts	▶ use a guiding mathematics framework to discuss the mathematical content in artifacts
▶ ground interpretations of thinking in evidence from artifacts	▶ compare/contrast different representations of mathematical ideas captured in artifacts
▶ generate plausible alternative interpretations of thinking and justifying ideas with evidence	▶ compare/contrast mathematical explanations and solution methods represented in artifacts
▶ see strengths (not just weaknesses) in thinking and understanding captured in artifacts	▶ use the exploration of mathematics to develop/engage norms of mathematical argument

Source: Adapted from Nikula, J., Goldsmith, L. T., Blasi, Z. V., & Seago, N. (2006). A framework for the strategic use of classroom artifacts in mathematics professional development. *NCSM Journal, 9*(1), p. 59.

as they did. The entries in the "Attention to Content" column help keep instruction focused on developing students' conceptual understanding and mathematical habits of mind. (This doesn't mean that you should ignore students' acquisition of facts and skills; rather, you should see them as important tools for supporting conceptual understanding and problem solving. And, of course, we should recognize that one student's "simple fact" may, for another student, be a developing idea.)

The exercises in each of the chapters that follow provide the opportunity to explore the two main components of the framework, using a variety of different artifacts. We hope that as you work through this book, you will begin to internalize the ideas in the framework and develop the disposition to approach your teaching with new lenses for considering artifacts from your own practice.

Section 1
Attention to Thinking

Skillful Use of Artifacts	
SKILLFUL USE OF ARTIFACTS INVOLVES:	
Attention to Thinking	**Attention to Content**
▶ distinguish between description and interpretation of work represented in artifacts	▶ use a guiding mathematical framework to discuss the mathematical content in artifacts
▶ ground interpretations of thinking in evidence from artifacts	▶ compare/contrast different representations of mathematical ideas captured in artifacts
▶ generate plausible alternative interpretations of thinking and justify ideas with evidence	▶ compare/contrast mathematical explanations and solution methods represented in artifacts
▶ see strengths (not just weaknesses) in thinking and understanding captured in artifacts	▶ use the exploration of mathematics to develop/engage norms of mathematical argument

Source: Adapted from Nikula, J., Goldsmith, L. T., Blasi, Z. V., & Seago, N. (2006). A framework for the strategic use of classroom artifacts in mathematics professional development. *NCSM Journal, 9*(1), 59.

In this section, we consider the left-hand column of the Skillful Use of Artifacts framework, focusing on classroom artifacts as data about students' thinking. In some ways, it's artificial to try to distinguish between examining artifacts in terms of thinking and content because in the end we're interested in both. The purpose of analyzing artifacts is ultimately to get a fuller picture of students' thinking *about particular content.* So, while organizing the work into a section on attention to thinking and another on attention to content is a bit artificial, we need to disentangle them at least temporarily in order to study these two important components in more detail. Since we have to start somewhere, we decided to begin with attention to thinking because, in the end, teaching is fundamentally about helping students to think more powerfully.

Both of the chapters in this section are designed to support greater attention to the specifics of students' mathematical thinking. Chapter 2 focuses on describing the work captured by artifacts and on using those descriptions as evidence for interpretations of students'

mathematical thinking. The process of gathering and interpreting evidence is core to instruction. Eliciting and interpreting evidence of students' understanding, for example, lies at the heart of formative assessment practices. Teachers base their instructional decision making and feedback to students largely on the information they gather about students thinking (Black, Harrison, Lee, Marshall, & Wiliam, 2003; Black & Wiliam, 1998; Heritage, 2010).

Chapter 3 concentrates on attending to the strengths as well as the weaknesses in students' mathematical thinking. Many teachers spend much of their energy figuring out what students don't yet know or can't yet do in order to fix erroneous thinking. This approach doesn't always leave room for teachers to see the potential in their students' thinking, even if that thinking is incorrect. And since we actually address students' deficiencies by building out from what they do know, it's important to become as inclined to recognize and utilize students' strengths as it is to attend to their weaknesses.

Describing and Interpreting Classroom Artifacts

Fifteen teachers sat around a table in the library at their monthly after-school professional development seminar. Mark, the group's facilitator, passed out five samples of students' work on the Crossing the River problem:

> Eight adults and two children need to cross a river, and they have one small boat. The boat can hold either one adult or one or two children. Everyone in the group is able to row the boat. How many one-way trips does it take for the eight adults and two children to cross the river? Write a rule for *n* adults and two children.

The teachers were familiar with the problem, having worked it themselves the month before. Mark stopped by one group just as Lorena picked up Linda's paper.

Linda hadn't written an algebraic expression, but she had diagramed an algorithm, using different-colored pencils to indicate trips to and from the opposite side of the river. Lorena glanced at Linda's work and noted, "This student is learning disabled," then moved on to the next work sample. Mark stepped into the conversation. "Lorena, your comment sounds like an interpretation of Linda's work, not a description of it. But you haven't said what evidence you're basing your comment on. What did you notice about Linda's work that led you to your interpretation?"

Lorena hesitated a moment and then explained, "Well, I've worked with lots of kids with learning disabilities, and lots of them have trouble with math. For one thing, they need extra help to stay organized enough to even figure out what they're supposed to be doing. So using colored pencils to keep track of her solution is the kind of thing I've seen lots of students with learning disabilities do."

In this vignette, Lorena's labeling of Linda as learning disabled is based on scanty evidence. As Mark pointed out to her, it's a big interpretive leap to go from "Linda used color to keep track of different kinds of trips" to "Linda's learning disabled"—a leap that seems unwarranted without further, thoughtful consideration of evidence from her work. Yet Lorena's tendency to categorize and label is something that we all do. In fact, it would be hard to get through the day *without* making connections between new experiences and old ones. Categorizing our experiences is a cognitive tool that can help keep us from being overwhelmed by the variety of information and situations we encounter daily.

In the classroom, for example, we are continually being called on to quickly size up students' work and respond to it. Unless we have a cache of experiences to draw on to help us make sense of students' work, each encounter with a student would require starting the process of sizing up and responding from scratch. Thinking of students in terms of certain categories—mathematically talented, hardworking, easily distracted, or even learning disabled—can help shape our in-the-moment responses to students as well as our broader learning goals and lesson plans.

But in school, as in life, categorizing and labeling has its hazards. If we make assessments on the basis of too little information, we can label students inaccurately (and sometimes unfairly). How likely does it seem to you that Lorena's characterization of Linda would actually hold water? What other possible interpretations might one reasonably make for Linda's choice to color code her solution strategy?

Part of the hazard of labeling is that once we've placed someone in a particular category, we filter and interpret our subsequent experiences with that person in terms of that category, glossing over (or even entirely failing to recognize) important information that doesn't fit with our expectations. After identifying Linda as learning disabled, Lorena seemed to feel that she'd adequately accounted for Linda's work even though she hadn't actually tried to understand Linda's mathematical thinking about the problem at all. Could it be that, instead of being organizationally challenged, Linda had a hunch that the solution to the problem depended on separating out trips taken by adults and children and that the color coding was an insightful and sophisticated way of playing out her intuition? Categories can obscure as well as reveal.

In this chapter, we practice suspending the tendency to categorize by focusing on first describing students' mathematical work and then interpreting the mathematical thinking that might be behind it.

Why Focus on Evidence?

We're wired as humans to interpret what we perceive. Like Lorena, we tend to fold descriptions of what we observe into our interpretations of the observations, often skipping over the evidence on which we based our assessments. When we do this, we often treat interpretations as if they were fact without necessarily even noticing that we've made the leap from describing to interpreting. Despite the tendency to merge these two processes, there are several advantages to being deliberate about distinguishing—and separating—description from interpretation when we examine classroom artifacts. For one, when we identify the evidence on which we base our interpretations, we can critically examine the bases for our claims—and make it possible for others to understand how we arrived at our interpretations.

Another reason to focus on grounding interpretations of classroom artifacts in evidence is that sticking close to the evidence helps to sharpen your focus on the specifics of students' mathematical thinking. The more practice you get at describing the particulars of students' work and interpreting the thinking that was likely to produce it, the better you'll get at seeing subtleties in students' thinking and at identifying the strengths as well as the weaknesses in their ideas. Since a big part of our jobs as teachers is to figure out what our students do and don't understand, being able to hone in on important aspects of their thinking is central to promoting further learning. We don't want to spend a lot of time working on mathematics that students already grasp, nor do we want lessons to whiz over their heads because we think they are grasping ideas when they're actually barely hanging on.

Of course, the idea of attending to what your students do and don't know isn't likely to be new to you—you look for information about whether your students are "getting it" on a regular basis. What might be new is going beyond checking whether a student's work is correct or not, taking a deeper look at *how* students seem to be thinking and *why* they might be doing so. Or maybe even this perspective isn't new, but the chance to get more practice using the perspective is what will motivate your work in this chapter.

Creating a Description of Student Work

There are several reasons to practice describing students' work. One is that it helps to sharpen your focus on the important mathematical ideas of a lesson. In some cases, sharpening this focus might involve actually analyzing mathematics that seem simple to us as adults but that are actually rather complex and sophisticated for those students who are just learning it. (For example, think about how it is entirely second nature for adults to accurately count a group of objects. Then remember that Piaget demonstrated over 75 years ago that a major cognitive accomplishment of the young child is the discovery of the one-to-one correspondence necessary for counting [Piaget & Szeminska, 1952].)

A second reason to practice describing students' work is that it hones your ability to recognize mathematically important elements in the work itself. We often assume that a correct answer means that students understood the relevant mathematical ideas and/ or procedures, and we often further assume that correct answers mean that our students think about the math the same way that we do. Both of these assumptions can contribute to a mind-set that leads to our overlooking (or failing to gather) information relevant to students' mathematical understanding.

In fact, students often think about mathematical situations differently than we do. For example, while adults typically use subtraction to solve "unknown addend" problems like the one below, primary school children frequently use addition. Ask a colleague to tell you how he or she figured out the answer for the following problem:

> Apriel wants to read 15 books over the summer. So far, she's read seven books. How many does she still have to read to reach her goal?

Chances are, your colleague subtracted 7 from 15 to get 8. If you ask second graders to solve the same problem, many of them will either count up from 7 to get 15 or ask themselves "what plus 7 makes 15?"

It's therefore useful for us, as teachers, to practice looking for aspects of students' thinking that are different from those of adults. Sometimes students simply have different ways of solving problems; sometimes their approaches may not seem elegant or even all that sensible from an adult perspective but nonetheless have a certain mathematical logic and coherence for the student, whose ideas are still under development. The importance of understanding the developmental trajectories of students' mathematical thinking and the value of learning to recognize and characterize evidence of developing thinking in students' work underlies the work of many mathematics educators and researchers (Carpenter, Franke, & Levi, 2003; Fosnot & Dolk, 2001; Mason, 2002; Schifter, 1996; Schifter, Bastable, & Russell, 2010a, 2010b [and other titles in the *Developing Mathematical Ideas* series]; Sherin, Jacobs, & Philipp, 2011; Stein, Smith, Henningsen, & Silver, 2009).

A third reason for describing students' work is that it provides evidence you can use in interpreting student understanding—and in considering whether you agree with others' interpretations. A description should be objective; different people should be able to agree on a description. Consider, for example, third-grader Nate's solution to the problem "20 paws. How many cats?" (see Figure 2.1).

Everyone should be able to agree that Nate drew a picture of four cats, that each cat has four legs, and that his answer to the question "How many cats" was 5. We might *wonder* about why he drew four and answered "five," and we can even offer some conjectures. (Maybe he drew four cats, counted paws, and knew that he needed only one cat's worth of paws more, so he didn't bother drawing the last cat. Or perhaps he made tally marks on scratch paper to find his answer but made a mistake when representing his solution on the worksheet. Or maybe Nate felt unsure of his own answer, which was actually four cats,

F i g u r e   2 . 1   Nate's solution

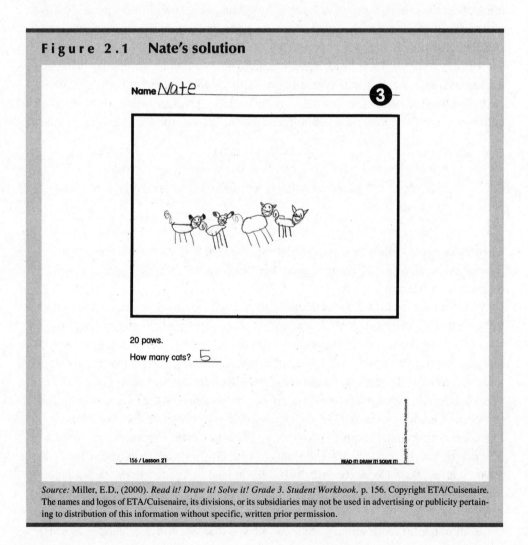

and wrote "5" because that was his table partner Ellen's answer, and Ellen usually gets answers right in math class.) At the point of making such conjectures, though, we are moving away from a simple description to possible *interpretations* of Nate's thinking. Describing his work should remain in the realm of the observable, not in the realm of speculation.

Creating a description of a student's work is also different than creating a blow-by-blow narrative of every feature of it. For our purposes here, we don't want to know *everything* that a student did; we want a description of those aspects of the solution that are relevant to students' mathematical thinking. For example, we don't need to note that Nate drew smiling cats with curly tails and spiky whiskers (although these features do make his work particularly endearing).

Since we're looking to tie the elements of the description to the key mathematical ideas and skills that underlie the problem, it's of central importance to understand what the key mathematical ideas and skills *are*. Therefore, the first step in describing students' work is to be clear about the mathematics at play in the problem. The more developed your understanding of the mathematics is, the more you will be able to capture the highlights of the mathematical ideas and skills you see the student calling on. You can then use your descriptions of the work to provide evidence for your interpretation of students' understanding of the relevant mathematics.

We've included a variety of exercises in this chapter so you can practice describing and interpreting students' thinking using different kinds of artifacts. We'll start with a relatively simple one—a written vignette that describes a student working on a problem. Exercise 2 is also relatively simple—a short video clip of a student solving a single problem. Exercise 3 uses students' written solutions to a word problem. We've also included two additional video-based exercises at the end of the chapter (Exercises 4 and 5). These exercises provide you with more experience analyzing videos of students at work.

Exercise 1: Danny

Imagine that you are watching a 5-year-old kindergartner named Danny work on the problem his teacher has just posed for the class:

> If there are seven children on the playground and eight more come over to play, how many children are there on the playground?

Here's what you see:

Danny and his table-mates James, Ben, and Ellen work individually. Each table has containers of snap cubes, base-10 blocks, popsicle sticks, and counting bears for children to use. Danny hums to himself as he grabs several handfuls of snap cubes. He comments that he's got a lot of red cubes and not so many yellows. He silently moves cubes from the big pile to a smaller grouping; when he's got seven, he stops and pushes them together into a bunch to his right. He looks back at the problem and then pulls out eight more from the larger pile. He pushes these eight together and puts the remaining snap cubes back in the container.

Danny looks over at James, who has made two piles of counting bears and is counting the second pile, softly saying "11, 12 . . ." Danny tells James, "I'm gonna make a snake out of mine!" as he begins lining up the snap cubes from the pile of eight. "Now I'm making it longer!" he says as he adds cubes from the pile of seven. He doesn't snap the cubes together as he makes his "snake," but he does make sure that each cube he adds touches its neighbor. He occasionally straightens the line as he continues to add the cubes from the second pile. When he is done, he counts the line of snap cubes, beginning with the leftmost one. He touches each as he counts aloud. Danny skips over the 11th cube, counts to 14, and writes ⎰⊬⎱ on his worksheet.

Now follow the steps below to first build a mathematically focused description of his work and then use the description to draw some interpretations of what Danny does—and perhaps doesn't—understand.

Process for Analyzing Danny's Work. The process outlined below is one we will use in analyzing all the classroom artifacts in this book. In general, throughout the book we first ask you to consider the math that is captured in the artifact and then to work with the artifact itself. In the case of this practice exercise, the artifact is the vignette depicting Danny's work. Follow the steps below to complete the exercise. Read through all the steps before you begin in order to get an overview of the process.

Step 1:
Identify key
math ideas
and skills.

Step 2:
Describe
Danny's
work.

Step 3: Use
evidence
to build an
interpretation.

Step 4:
Reflect on
your work.

Step 1: **Identify key math ideas and skills.** Ask yourself about what a kindergartner has to know to solve the playground problem. Try to be more specific than "he has to know addition" or "he has to know his number facts."

Step 2: **Describe Danny's work.** Reread the vignette, looking for the parts that seem relevant to how Danny solved the problem (you may want to underline them). Use them to build a description of Danny's solution strategy.

Step 3: **Use evidence to build an interpretation.** How would you interpret Danny's thinking? Use the portions of the description you highlighted as evidence for your ideas about how Danny's mathematical understanding connects to the key ideas you identified earlier.

Step 4: **Reflect on your work.** If you are working with others, take a few minutes to share and discuss your descriptions of Danny's work. Be sure you can support your descriptions with evidence from the vignette. Use the study questions on page 21 to help you reflect on your work (and, if you are working with others, to start your discussion). You can also refer to the commentary that follows to stimulate your reflections and discussion.

Study Questions

► What aspects of the vignette did you include in your description?

► How did the aspects you included connect to the key mathematical ideas you identified?

► How did you interpret Danny's thinking?

  ▪ What do you think he understood and was able to do?

  ▪ What do you think is still under development for Danny?

► What aspects of the vignette did you exclude? What about them made you exclude them from your description?

Commentary on Danny's Work. Below are thoughts about some of the key mathematical ideas that the "playground" problem taps and comments on how descriptions of Danny's work can support interpretations of his mathematical thinking with respect to these key ideas.

Key mathematical ideas. For young children like Danny, an important idea that's not directly related to counting or addition is the more general notion that you can represent one situation with another. In this case, the idea is that objects like snap cubes or counting bears (or even marks on a paper) can stand in for the children on the playground. In addition, a number of ideas about counting and adding are likely to be relevant to his work on the problem:

CCSS—Kindergarten
Represent addition and subtraction with objects, fingers, mental images, drawings, [and other media]. p. 11.

- When you're counting the number of objects in a collection, the last number in your count tells you the number of objects (this is the idea of cardinality).

- You can think about addition as the joining of collections (subsets) of objects; the sum is the total number of objects in the new, joined set.

- The order in which you add sets doesn't make any difference (this is the commutative property of addition).

CCSS—Grade 1
Use addition and subtraction within 20 to solve word problems involving situations of adding to taking from, putting together, taking apart, and comparing, with unknowns in all positions. p. 15.

- You can add by starting with the size of one of the subsets and then continue objects. This is often called "counting on" (see Figure 2.2).

Figure 2.2 Counting on

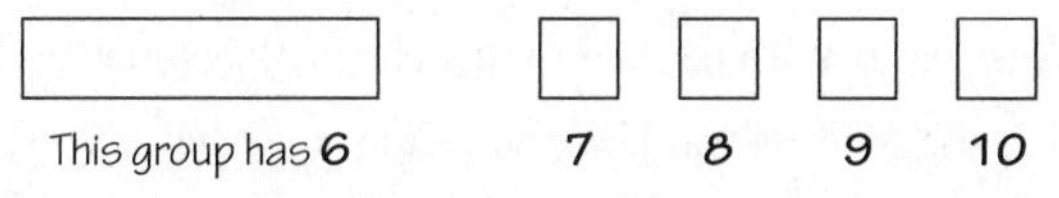

This group has 6   7   8   9   10

- It's more efficient to "add on" to the larger subset because you have fewer objects to count.
- Because addition involves joining sets in any order, you can also decompose and recompose sets (and numbers) into configurations that make for easy addition (this idea calls on both the associative and the commutative properties of addition). For example,

$$
\begin{aligned}
8 + 7 &= 8 + (5 + 2) \\
&= 8 + (2 + 5) \\
&= (8 + 2) + 5 \\
&= 10 + 5 \\
&= 15
\end{aligned}
$$

Description of Danny's work. Given that our goal in looking at Danny's work is to consider his understanding of the mathematics involved in the "playground" problem, we see the following aspects of the description as particularly relevant:

- He chooses a manipulative (snap cubes) to help model the problem.
- He accurately counts out the two groups representing the addends (a group of seven and a group of eight).
- He puts these two groups together, starting with the pile of eight blocks.
- He counts out the total, starting from "1."
- He miscounts the total.

We would *not* include the following in our description:

- He uses snap cubes instead of other available manipulatives. In some cases, choice of manipulatives might be important. If Danny were solving a problem using larger quantities, such as $47 + 78$, then his using snap cubes instead of base-10 blocks, for example, might suggest that he's not using knowledge of the structure of the number system to decompose the numbers into groupings that are easier to deal with ($40 + 7$ and $70 + 8$). Since Danny is working on a problem with small numbers here, his specific choice of manipulative is probably not all that informative.
- He begins his work by taking out a bunch of cubes, from which he counts out the set of seven and the set of eight. If we were examining Danny's estimation skills, this observation might be of central importance, but it seems less mathematically important for this problem.
- He comments on the color of the cubes.
- He comments to James about making a snake.
- He makes sure that, as he lines up the cubes, they touch each other.
- He writes the "4" backward. While Danny's teacher may want to help him write numbers correctly, his error is pretty common and isn't an issue about his understanding of mathematical ideas.

CCSS—Kindergarten

Understand addition as putting together and adding to . . . p. 10.

Understand that the last number name said tells the number of objects counted. The number of objects is the same regardless of their arrangement or the order in which they were counted. p. 10.

Understand the relationship between numbers and quantities; connect counting to cardinality. p. 11.

CCSS—Grade 1

Understand and apply properties of operations . . . p. 14.

Interpretation of Danny's work. While the purpose of describing students' work is to provide an evidentiary base for interpreting their thinking, you have probably noticed that there's some element of interpretation happening even during the step of creating a description. This is inevitable (as we've been emphasizing) since what you notice is influenced by what you know. Our goal in describing his work is to have evidence that will support our interpretations of the strengths and possible limitations of his understanding about number and operations.

His accurate counting out of the group of seven and the group of eight, for example, suggests that he has come some way toward mastery of key ideas about counting (one-to-one correspondence, ordinality, and cardinality). We don't know how accurately he can count larger numbers, but he seems to get the idea that each object gets counted once and that each count has to be associated with a number. Given that Danny seems comfortable and competent with counting, we would focus our attention on how he's building an understanding of addition.

We think that his process of reorganizing the separate sets of blocks into a single group suggests that he understands that addition can be thought of as joining sets. However, the fact that he finds the total by recounting *all* of the blocks suggests that Danny doesn't yet understand that he can use the cardinality of one set as the starting place for "counting on" the second set. Given his accurate counting of the groups of seven and eight, his miscount of the total may be a "careless" error, or it may be an indication that keeping track of the correspondence between number and object gets strained when the set he's counting is somewhat larger—say, greater than 10 or so. We'd be curious to see whether he could accurately recount the blocks in his snake or perhaps another, somewhat smaller group of maybe 12 or 13 objects.

Danny's work doesn't offer evidence of his having addition strategies based on number facts, so we might also want to explore this. We could, for example, ask him whether he could think of any other ways to solve the problem and keep an eye out for whether he offered strategies that relied on decomposing and recomposing numbers—or whether he understood such strategies when suggested by someone else (e.g., finding combinations of 10 or using doubles).

Exercise 2: Melissa

Exercise 2 is based on a video clip of a portion of an interview with Melissa, a fifth grader. In this short clip, Melissa compares an improper fraction $\left(\frac{5}{3}\right)$ and a mixed number $\left(1\frac{2}{3}\right)$.

Typically, when we talk about working with video artifacts we mean footage of classroom work—whole-class discussions, for example, or excerpts of small-group work. Because we want you to have the chance to zero in on students' thinking with a minimum of distraction for these first video exercises, we've chosen video of individual students.

The video, as well as the videos for Exercises 4 and 5 at the end of the chapter, capture a portion of a one-on-one "math interviews" with elementary students. These interviews were specifically designed to elicit students' thinking as they solved problems, not to help students get correct answers or fix errors they might have made during the course of their problem solving. Because the interviews were explicitly about *not* affecting the students' thinking, the video captures a kind of interaction that you may find foreign. In fact, the goal of "just" listening for students' ideas rather than of intervening to promote learning may strike you as decidedly unteacherly. But if you think about it, it's hard to be a responsive teacher without taking the time to understand how your students are actually thinking. In your own classroom, you probably check in informally with your students on a fairly regular basis as they work, waiting to make comments or suggestions or to pose challenges until you get a sense of how they're approaching a task. Similarly, when students come to you for help, you probably take a minute to gather some information about how they've already approached the problem or what they find difficult or confusing before you weigh in. It's that "data gathering" mind-set rather than an "intervening" one that we're tapping into in the video exercises.

Process for Viewing and Analyzing the *Melissa* Video. Follow the steps below as you complete the exercise. Read through all the steps before you begin in order to get an overview of the process.

Step 1: Identify key math ideas.

Step 2: Prepare to watch the video.

Step 3: View the *Melissa* clip.

Step 1: Identify key math ideas. Take a few minutes to think about Melissa's task $\left(\text{compare } \frac{5}{3} \text{ and } 1\frac{2}{3}\right)$. What are important mathematical ideas involved in representing numbers as improper and mixed fractions and in comparing them? What kinds of difficulties might you expect students to encounter when making such comparisons?

Step 2: Prepare to watch the video. Make a copy of the blank Chapter 2 worksheet (see Figure 2.3; a blank worksheet is located in the Appendix and as a writeable PDF on PDToolKit). Think about the kind of information you'll need to collect to fill out the worksheet; have some paper on hand for making notes about the details of Melissa's work as you watch the video.

Step 3: View the *Melissa* clip. Find the *Melissa* clip on PDToolKit and watch it at least once. Remember that your purpose in viewing the video is to practice describing and interpreting Melissa's work; you may want to make notes while you're viewing to remember things that seem particularly interesting or important. If you do, be sure to note the associated time code on the video clip so that you can easily refer back to your evidence.

F i g u r e 2 . 3   Blank Chapter 2 worksheet

Chapter 2 Worksheet: Describing and Interpreting Artifacts

Key Mathematical Ideas:

My Descriptions	My interpretations and supporting evidence	Alternative interpretations?	Questions I'd like to ask

Step 4: **Complete the "My Descriptions" column of the worksheet.** Remember that your goal here is to describe, objectively, what Melissa does (and says) that you think is relevant to her understanding of the math. You may want to replay segments of the video or even watch it through a second time from beginning to end—Melissa's explanation goes by pretty quickly, and there might be parts of it that you'd like to revisit as you complete the worksheet. You can also refer to the video transcript (Figure 2.4) as you complete the worksheet.

Step 5: **Complete the "My Interpretations" column of the worksheet.** Use the "My Descriptions" column to provide evidence for your interpretations.

Step 6: **Complete the rest of the worksheet.** See if you can come up with alternative interpretations for Melissa's work. Often, generating alternatives helps us think more broadly about a student's knowledge and skill. Think, too, about questions that Melissa's work raises for you: what do you wonder about her math understanding? What questions would you like to ask her?

Step 4:
Complete the "My Descriptions" column of the worksheet.

Step 5:
Complete the "My Interpretations" column of the worksheet.

Step 6:
Complete the rest of the worksheet.

FIGURE 2.4

Transcript of **Melissa** Video

Interviewer:	Can you say those two for me?
Melissa:	Five thirds and one and two thirds.
Interviewer:	Okay.
Melissa:	And I think they're equal. Because that's five thirds, and I was thinking maybe times those together, or divide them. That's two. I said, "Five times 3 is 15." So I thought maybe that's 5, and that's 1. One, one, five here. Fifteen. And then that's—times those together, and that's 5. I mean, 15.
Interviewer:	Oh, okay. So you multiplied 3 times—
Melissa:	Five.
Interviewer:	Five.
Melissa:	And that's fifteen.
Interviewer:	Fifteen.
Melissa:	Is equal to. And then 1, and plus these—add these together.
Interviewer:	You added those two.
Melissa:	And that's 15.
Interviewer:	Okay, very good.

Source: Philipp, R., Cabral, C., & Schappelle, B. (2011). *Searchable IMAP Video Collection: Children's Mathematical Thinking Clips* Copyright © 2011 by San Diego State University Research Foundation. All rights reserved except those explicitly licensed to Pearson Education, Inc. Video and transcript were created during IMAP project by Randolph Philipp, Bonnie Schappelle and Candace Cabral.

Step 7:
Reflect on your work.

Step 7: Reflect on your work. If you are working with others, take a few minutes to share and discuss your descriptions and interpretations. Be sure to support your interpretations with evidence from the video—your notes and worksheet comments will help you do this. Use the study questions on page 27 to help you reflect on your observations (and, if you are working with others, to start your discussion). You can also use the completed sample worksheet (Table 2.1 on page 28) to help you think about your own responses and to stimulate your reflections and discussion.

Study Questions

▶ What aspects of Melissa's work did you include in your description? What details did you intentionally leave out?

▶ What evidence did you use in formulating your interpretations of her math understanding?

▶ What alternative interpretations did you make?

▶ What were some strengths and weaknesses you found in Melissa's work?

▶ What do you think she does and doesn't understand?

▶ If you had been the interviewer, what questions would you have liked to ask Melissa to find out more about her thinking?

Commentary on Melissa's Interview. This video clip may serve as a reminder that students may answer problems correctly even though their reasoning is faulty (and vice versa—they may also get problems wrong even if their basic conceptual reasoning is sound). It can also serve as a reminder that many of us have a tendency to "fill in the blanks" of another person's thinking, making the assumption that they think the same way we do and that correct answers imply correct thinking. If the interviewer had simply accepted Melissa's solution without probing her thinking, it would have been tempting to conclude that she had a clear and mature understanding of how to move between different representations of fractions larger than one— she did not hesitate as she named both numbers and offered her observation that they were equal to the interviewer without prompting. This clip reminds us of the importance of holding the "correct answers = correct thinking" assumption at bay and checking in with students to make sure that correct answers do indeed reflect solid mathematical thinking.

Key mathematical ideas. We see the following mathematical ideas as relevant for Melissa's task (see also Table 2.1).

- There are many different ways to represent a number.

- In writing a fraction, the denominator represents the number of parts into which a whole has been equally divided; the numerator represents how many parts of the whole are under consideration.

- Whole numbers can be expressed as a fraction. For example, $\frac{3}{3} = \frac{4}{4} = \frac{240}{240} = 1$.

- When we write an improper fraction like $\frac{5}{3}$, we mean "five one-thirds," or $\frac{1}{3} + \frac{1}{3} + \frac{1}{3} + \frac{1}{3} + \frac{1}{3}$.

CCSS—Grade 3
Develop understanding of fractions as numbers. p. 22.

CCSS—Grade 4
Extend understanding of fraction equivalence and ordering. p. 28.
Build fractions from unit fractions by applying and extending previous understandings of operations with whole numbers. p. 30.

TABLE 2.1 Completed Sample Worksheet: *Melissa* Video

Key Mathematical Ideas:	• There are many different ways to represent a number. • In writing a fraction, the denominator represents the number of parts into which a whole has been equally divided; the numerator represents how many parts of the whole are under consideration. • Whole numbers can be expressed as a fraction. • When we write an improper fraction like $\frac{5}{3}$, we mean "five one-thirds."		
My Descriptions	**My Interpretations and Supporting Evidence**	**Alternative Interpretations?**	**My Questions**
Melissa reads both numbers without hesitation.	She's familiar with fractions.		
She says that she thinks the numbers are equal and then goes on to explain her thinking without prompting.	Until Melissa offered her explanation, it seemed that she knew that the two numbers were equal. Generally, lack of hesitation suggests that someone is confident of their ideas; is this a good interpretation in this case—does that tiny laugh suggest lack of certainty in her work/ answer?	She anticipated that the interviewer would want her to explain her answer. She might be a quick thinker —she comes up with an explanation on the spot that manages to "find" a 15 on both sides of the equals sign even though the explanation does not make sense mathematically.	How confident is Melissa of her answer? Is she used to thinking through (and explaining) her answers in school? Does she know that she's provided an explanation that isn't mathematically valid? Is she troubled by it? (What does her lack of hesitation mean in terms of her own attention to mathematical ideas and concepts?)
She says that you might multiply or divide the $\frac{5}{3}$.	She's trying to remember what her teacher told her about how to compare fractions.	She's thinking about how to put each number into a form that will allow comparison.	What does she understand about the meaning of the value in the numerator and in the denominator? Does she understand that $1 = \frac{3}{3}$? Could she represent these values with drawings or manipulatives?
After she talks about multiplying/dividing, she says "that's two."			What did she mean by "that's two"? (Or was it maybe "that's *too*," even though it didn't seem like she was making a comparison or starting a sentence that she didn't finish?) Is this statement mathematically important?
She gets 15 with the mixed number by adding the 2 and 3 from the $\frac{2}{3}$ and writing the 5 to the right of the 1 from the mixed number.	She doesn't seem to be engaging her sense making here and is either ignoring what she knows about place value or is confused about the value of the digits—she treats the "1" in $1\frac{2}{3}$ as both a unit and a 10 (when she renames the number 15). She doesn't seem to see either fraction $\left(\frac{5}{3} \text{ or } \frac{2}{3}\right)$ as representing a value itself but as made up of two individual parts (numerator and denominator) that can be operated on (multiplying in one case and adding in the other).	She doesn't remember the algorithm and is trying to recall the operations she's been told to use—she knows that when you rename fractions, you do some combination of multiplying and adding, so that's what she's doing.	Does Melissa think that math can make sense? Is her difficulty deeply conceptual, or is she "just" having trouble with the notation and "naked" computation? Would she be able to represent and compare $\frac{5}{3}$ and $1\frac{2}{3}$ if she'd been asked to draw them with diagrams or build them with objects?

Description of Melissa's work. We see the following aspects of Melissa's work as salient in terms of her mathematical understanding and skill (see also the sample worksheet).

- Melissa doesn't hesitate to engage in the problem.

- On her own initiative, Melissa states that the two quantities are equal and offers a reason.

- She multiplies numerator and denominator of the improper fraction (to get 15) but adds the numerator and denominator portion of the mixed number (to get 5).

- She rewrites the mixed number, writing the 1 and then the 5 (which she got from adding numerator and denominator) and says "15."

Interpretations (with evidence) and questions about Melissa's work. We were left with a lot more questions about Melissa's understanding than we were with interpretations of it. That said, we do have two interpretations to offer—perhaps you had others of your own.

- The ease with which she reads the two numbers and volunteers the fact that they are equal suggests that Melissa has some familiarity with fractions and that she understands that they can be named in different ways. She may also understand that it's possible to describe a quantity in terms of a fraction that's larger than 1.

- Melissa's explanation suggests that she's encountered but not mastered the algorithms for converting mixed numbers to improper fractions and vice versa: she starts her work by saying she needs to multiply (or maybe divide). She then renames $\frac{5}{3}$ by multiplying numerator and denominator (5×3); later on, she adds numerator and denominator ($2 + 3$) from the mixed number. These are operations that are part of the "conversion" algorithms for mixed and improper fractions, but the way she uses them lacks a mathematical logic. She operates on both numbers $\left(\frac{5}{3} \text{ and } 1\frac{2}{3}\right)$ to demonstrate equivalence rather than leaving one as is and working on the other in order to express both numbers in the same form—either two mixed numbers or two improper fractions. She also operates on numerator and denominator differently in the two cases and seems to be performing computations on any of the numbers that will make the equivalence "come out." She doesn't hesitate as she offers her explanation, but as she proceeds, she looks at the camera in a way that could be interpreted as self-conscious.

After observing Melissa's video, we're left with the following questions about what she might and might not understand:

- Is Melissa aware of the lack of logic to her answer?

- Does she have the expectation that her math work should make sense?

- This short clip of Melissa's work doesn't allow us much insight into what she understands about fractions more generally. Some possible follow-up questions about her understanding could include the following:

> **CCSS—Mathematical Practice**
>
> Make sense of problems and persevere in solving them. p. 6.

- Can she identify equivalent *proper* fractions when they are presented numerically?

- Does she understand that $1 = \frac{3}{3}$?

- Can she accurately draw (or build with manipulatives) representations of $\frac{5}{3}$ and $1\frac{2}{3}$? If so, can she accurately compare these?

Reflecting on Exercise 2. Take a minute to think about your work on this exercise. Were you able to separate out descriptions of Melissa's mathematical work from interpretations of her thinking? Were you able to support your interpretations with evidence?

We want you to focus on the distinction between description and interpretation because we want you to get used to recognizing where, in your own work with students, you're making decisions based on evidence about their thinking and where you're filling in those blanks and making decisions based on your assumptions about their understanding. Teachers can't do their work without interpreting their students' work, but it's important to *check* these interpretations. We want to neither overestimate our students' understanding—as someone might have done with Melissa—nor underestimate it.

Using Artifacts in Your Own Classroom

We'll return to collecting video-based artifacts at the end of this section, but first want to highlight some kinds of data that you can consider collecting as part of activities that are already part of your regular instruction and require little or no extra effort to gather. Below are two examples of classroom activities that can yield artifacts to mine for data about your students' thinking; we're sure that you will think of other kinds of artifacts that can be informative as well.

Warm-Ups

Does your textbook suggest a warm-up activity at the beginning of a lesson? Warm-ups are a nice time for practice, review, or as a lead-in to the main part of your lesson. They can also offer you an opportunity to do some quick checks on the robustness of students' skill and knowledge. If you use warm-ups that involve written work, you can collect students' papers and review them more carefully after class (see the next section below). If warm-ups are oral, you can still jot down notes about interesting or surprising responses—answers that seem way off, for example, or common errors that you find students making. You can use these notes to reflect on the strengths and weaknesses you see in students' responses and to use these observations to support future planning.

It may be tempting to try to fix issues that emerge during a warm-up right then and there, but this will take time away from your main lesson by turning the warm-up into a lesson of its own. Instead, think about using the warm-up to keep track of concepts or skills that you feel you need to revisit in future classes or on a more individual basis with particular students.

Homework, Quizzes, and Tests

The triumvirate of homework, quizzes, and tests offers you a constant stream of data about your students. In addition to providing information about whether students are doing their assignments, whether they seem to be studying for exams, and how well they are performing, with a little extra work on your part you can use homework, quizzes, and tests to get a sense of the *kind* of thinking students are applying to their work.

For example, try taking a homework assignment (or a quiz or test) and sorting the papers into three piles: a "gets the idea" pile, a "somewhat gets it" pile, and a pile for students who seem to be really struggling (or whose solutions raise lots of questions for you). Which pile is the largest? Is it the pile that you expected? If so, you probably have a pretty solid grasp of students' understanding. It's not uncommon, though, for teachers to think that students have a better handle on the math they're been studying than they really do. It can be somewhat surprising to find that it's the second or third piles that are bigger than the first or second. You can give this sorting a try in Exercise 3, where you'll practice with the homework samples from a fourth-grade class.

Looking for similarities and differences in solution strategies can help teachers understand students' thinking.

Exercise 3: Sorting Homework

The work you'll use in this exercise was collected from fourth-grade students in February, about halfway through the school year. They were asked to solve the following word problem:

> Carolyn's mom brought eight brownies to Carolyn's dance group. That day six girls were there. If they share the brownies equally, how much does each girl get?

(The structure of the problem is identical to the one Myrna works on in Exercise 5.)

Process for Sorting the Homework Samples. Follow the steps below as you complete the exercise. Read through all the steps before you begin in order to get an overview of the process.

Step 1:
Identify key
math ideas.

Step 2:
Study the
student work
samples.

Step 3:
Sort the work
samples.

Step 4:
Refine your
sorts into
subpiles.

Step 5:
Reflect on
your work.

Step 1: Identify key math ideas. Take a minute to think about the problem. What are the key mathematical ideas for fourth-grade students? How would you solve the problem? What might you expect the range of work to look like for a fourth-grade class?

Step 2: Study the student work samples. These are found in the Appendix and as PDFs on PDToolKit. You may want to make copies of the work samples or perhaps just take notes on the ones in the book. If you do the latter, you might find sticky notes useful. Be sure to make *brief* notes about your interpretation of each student's work and supporting descriptive evidence. With 14 work samples to consider, you don't need extensive notes, but you do want to remember what thoughts went into your sorting decisions.

Step 3: Sort the work samples. We suggest you try three piles: (1) basically gets it, (2) somewhat gets it, and (3) needs more work. However, if you have categories that you prefer, try those too. Make sure that you can justify your sorting decisions with evidence for your interpretations of students' work.

Step 4: Refine your sorts into subpiles. Now that you have done a rough sort, try sorting even further within each pile. A second sort will challenge you to be more explicit about the aspects of students' work that led you to your categorization. Look more carefully at the first pile. What kinds of differences do you see among this group of students, all of whom are basically able to successfully do the mathematics? For example, do you see differences in the representations that different students use, in the specifics of the approaches they take to their solutions, in the sophistication of their thinking, or in the care they take to check (and possibly correct) their work? Do the same for the other piles.

Step 5: **Reflect on your work.** If you're working with others, take a few minutes to share and discuss how you sorted the samples and why you did so. Be sure to support your interpretations with evidence from the work samples. Use the study questions below to help you reflect on your observations (and, if you are working with others, to start your discussion). We've also provided a short commentary below.

Study Questions

▶ What was your evidence for sorting work into particular piles?

▶ What's common to the work samples within a pile? What kinds of differences did you find?

▶ Do you feel that the second sort helped you make more fine-grained distinctions between students' likely thinking? For example, how did you sort Aiden, Andrew, Annie, Lexi, and Patrick? Were they all in the same pile on the first sort? Were they in the same subpiles on the second sort? Why or why not?

▶ How might you use this approach to quickly get a sense of *your* students' understanding?

Commentary on Exercise 3. The way someone sorts the work depends, of course, on his or her mathematical goals. One reasonable goal would be for students to find a solution where all the brownies are divided among the six girls—this goal requires expressing the solution as a fraction (or decimal). If you were to sort on the basis of this criterion, then your "gets it" pile might have included all solutions that were expressed as one brownie and a fraction of another (whether or not the answer was actually right or wrong), and your "needs more work" pile might include responses expressed in terms only of one brownie and a whole-number remainder. In this case, you might not have a "kind of gets it" pile with this group of students at all.

Your goal might have been more exacting. For example, you might have been looking for correct solutions expressed as mixed numbers or even solutions where the fraction was expressed in lowest terms. If so, then your "gets it" pile would be substantially smaller. But for any of these goals (and others, too), chances are that you were able to find enough commonality among students' work that you could sort them into a relatively small number of piles according to criteria based on levels of understanding division and/or fractions.

When you go one step further and refine your sorts into subcategories, you can begin to identify groups of students with common strengths and weaknesses in their understanding. This lets you think about how to provide other learning experiences for these groups that can be more specifically targeted to develop the weaknesses and build on their strengths. In this way, you can efficiently differentiate instruction. For example, Aiden's, Andrew's, and Annie's sketches of the problem solution all seem to demonstrate a conceptual understanding of the task, but their numerical answers suggest that they may have experienced some difficulty connecting different solution representations. If you were their teacher, you might think about a lesson or two that provide opportunities for these students to make these connections explicit.

Conducting a more careful analysis of students' work can potentially help you with another teaching challenge—deciding when it is okay to move on to another idea or topic. You can use the same analyses you've done to better understand the needs of individual students to help you think about the class as a whole. For example, you can ask yourself whether most of the students in the "needs more work" pile are the ones who are always pretty much playing catch-up or whether there are more students in this pile than is typical. If the latter is the case, you might want to spend more time consolidating students' understanding before moving on. Then again, you might feel that even the students who need more experiences have some basic understanding on which you could continue to build as you proceed with the curriculum, and you would decide to move on.

Regardless of your decision, as long as there are students in your class who are still struggling with the concept, you face the considerable challenge of figuring out what kinds of experiences you need to provide them so that they can continue learning the math. Your close observation and analysis of their work can help you plan additional learning opportunities that will go beyond "reteaching" to target specific requisite ideas and skills that need scaffolding or developing. (In many cases, reteaching is about as effective as trying to communicate with a non–English speaker by simply repeating what you've said, only slower and louder. Articulating more clearly and at a higher volume still isn't going to make things any more sensible to someone totally lacking knowledge of English. Similarly, retracing the same mathematical ground isn't likely to help students who are standing in an entirely different part of the mathematical landscape.)

When you take the extra time to closely examine an assignment, you can get a clearer sense of your students' progress and also those aspects of understanding and skill that still need developing. While a deeper analysis of students' work is a worthwhile use of time, you don't have to do it every day. This kind of analysis *does* take extra time, and we all know that teachers' time is at a premium. Instead, reserve your closer look at students' work for

CCSS—Mathematical Practices

Reason abstractly and quantitatively. p. 6.

Attend to precision. p. 7.

CCSS—Grade 3

Develop understanding of fractions as numbers. p. 24.

CCSS—Grade 4

Use the four operations with whole numbers to solve problems. p. 28.

Build fractions from unit fractions by applying and extending previous understandings of operations with whole numbers. p. 30.

CCSS—Grade 5

Solve word problems involving division of whole numbers leading to answers in the form of fractions or mixed numbers. p. 36.

an assignment that focuses on an idea you see as central to the current unit or make the time to reflect more deeply on a lesson that left you with questions about what your students were thinking. Instead of doing an exercise like this with work from the whole class, you might decide to examine the work of one or two students you're wondering about. (If you're wondering how students approached a particular task, you might make such a "depth sounding" a one-time event. If, on the other hand, you're not sure about a child's mathematical thinking across the board, you may want to collect that student's work on a more regular basis and analyze it over time to build a better understanding of his or her overall grasp of mathematical ideas and skills.) Remember, too, that the more practice you get in attending to students' ideas, the better you're likely to be in zeroing in on important thinking as it's happening in the bustle of classroom lessons.

Making Videos of Your Own

Because video can capture the math classroom in all of its dynamism and complexity, it offers an unparalleled opportunity to practice looking for students' mathematical thinking in a variety of classroom contexts—students working individually, solving problems in small groups, and sharing and discussing their work as a whole class. With video, you can capture students' solutions as they unfold over time and can inquire into both verbal and nonverbal elements of their problem solving. You can practice analyzing students' work in real time and can also slow the action down, stopping and revisiting aspects of the class as you see fit. The more video you study, the better you become at noticing the mathematically important details of students' work and at interpreting how these details reflect students' mathematical thinking. Working with video outside the classroom is great for developing an eye (and ear) for the mathematical thinking that goes on during class activities and discussions.

Now that video cameras are relatively inexpensive, it's pretty easy to make videos of your own lessons for later review and reflection. (In fact, if you have a cell phone that records video, you could even think about making short recordings with it.) This new video accessibility offers a wonderful opportunity to take a more careful look at the mathematical work that goes on in your class and to take more time to think about how to build toward greater student understanding in subsequent lessons. But working with video of your own classroom can also be distracting, so be prepared. You might find, for example, that it's hard to look past elements of your own teaching (or your haircut or your posture) to focus in on how students are working with the mathematical ideas of the lesson. Try to take the same generous and inquiring approach to your own class that we ask you to take throughout this book when analyzing the work of others. Remember, you're working with artifacts in order to learn to explore students' mathematical thinking more deeply and, by extension, to take advantage of this learning in your own teaching. This work is not about labeling or passing judgment on others or on ourselves.

We have a few technical suggestions about filming. You're likely to get more out of the video if you can focus the camera on different speakers during discussion and move about the room during individual and/or small-group work to capture some of the conversation and work in progress. If you can swing it, you might even try to round up several cameras so that you can set up a fixed camera to capture whole-group discussions and also have a roaming camera to capture individual or small-group work.

We also advise trying to get someone else to do the video recording if at all possible. With someone else as cameraperson, the video is likely to capture more of the work going on in the lesson because you don't have to add "filmmaker" to your other responsibilities. You'll be free to continue to function in your normal role as teacher while someone else documents the work. You might arrange a quid pro quo with another teacher in your building, videotaping his or her class in exchange for video of yours. Having a colleague do the videography (another teacher in the building or perhaps a math coach or specialist) has the added advantage of offering a new pair of eyes in the class and most likely a fresh look at your own students. You also gain the advantage of being able to discuss the lesson with another colleague who was there to experience it firsthand. If a colleague isn't available, you might try getting a video production student from a local high school.

If you can't arrange to get help with the videotaping, you can still set up a stationary camera someplace in the room where you can capture most of the action for whole-group work (include the board in the shot). If your lesson includes individual or small-group work, you may find a way to take the camera with you as you circulate. You might also think about videotaping one-on-one sessions with individual students, particularly if you're puzzled about how they're thinking or approaching their work.

Make sure that you also capture at least some of your students' written work as well, either recording work samples on camera or by taking notes. If you regularly use chart paper to record solutions, you're all set. Having the written work is often helpful for following students' comments—you might be surprised by how often students' verbal descriptions of their solutions use ambiguous referents (what is the "it" in "then I timesed it by . . .") and how much the corresponding written work can help to clarify some of the ambiguity.

Finally, you can use copies of the blank Chapter 2 worksheet to help you describe and interpret your students' mathematical thinking. Feel free to use it as is or to modify it to make it work better for you when describing and interpreting artifacts of your own. While you obviously have much more background knowledge about your own students and the history of their mathematical experiences in your class to inform your analysis, try to focus primarily on describing the mathematical work you see and on pointing to evidence in the artifact to support your interpretations of their thinking. What mathematical strengths do you see in your students? Weaknesses? What questions about their understanding would you like to pursue?

Wrapping Up

37

Chapter 2
**Describing
and Interpret-
ing Classroom
Artifacts**

The goal of this chapter is to help you to attend more closely to your students' mathematical thinking, distinguishing between making descriptions of their work and drawing interpretations of their understanding on the basis of evidence from those descriptions. Our research and that of others suggests that with practice, teachers learn to notice important and subtle aspects of their students' work and to become more adept at interpreting the thinking behind the work (Goldsmith & Seago, 2011; Santagata, Zannoni, & Sigler, 2007; Star & Strickland, 2008; van Es, 2011; van Es & Sherin, 2008). We hope that you will take the opportunities we present in this chapter, including the exercises following this section, to practice honing your skills.

Additional Exercises: Video Clips of Two Math Interviews

In these exercises, you'll work with video clips of two other math interviews to practice describing and interpreting student work. In Exercise 4, third-grader Kasage solves a multidigit addition problem; Myrna, a second grader, solves a division problem in Exercise 5. Both exercises include completed sample worksheets to support your work.

Exercise 4: Kasage

In this clip, Kasage, a third grader, works on the "naked" addition problem, $638 + 476$. The interviewer asks her to solve it using another student's strategy. The strategy involves working left to right and, presumably, is different from the one that Kasage uses spontaneously.

Process for Viewing and Analyzing the *Kasage* Video. Follow the steps below as you complete the exercise. Read through all the steps to get an overview of the process.

Step 1: **Identify key math ideas.** Take a few minutes to think about key mathematical ideas involved in adding multidigit numbers. What kind of understanding and skill are involved in doing the computation from left to right? What kinds of difficulties might you expect Kasage to encounter when using this strategy (which is likely not her own)?

Step 2: **Prepare to watch the video.** Make a copy of the blank Chapter 2 worksheet (located in the Appendix and as a writeable PDF on PDToolKit). Think about the kind of information you'll need to collect to fill out the worksheet; have some paper on hand for making notes about the details of Kasage's work as you watch the video.

Step 1:
Identify key
math ideas.

Step 2:
Prepare to
watch the
video.

PDToolkit
for
*Examining Mathematics
Practice through
Classroom Artifacts*

Step 3:
View the
Kasage clip.

Step 3: View the *Kasage* clip. Find the *Kasage* clip on PDToolKit and watch it at least once. Recall that your purpose in viewing the video is to practice describing and interpreting Kasage's work. You may want to view the clip once to get an overall sense of her work and a second time to gather more detail as you complete your worksheet. Keep scratch paper handy to jot down notes and time codes so that you can easily refer back to the evidence that you used to build your interpretations. We've included a transcript of the interview for you to supplement your video viewing (Figure 2.5); you may want to consult it while completing the worksheet.

FIGURE 2.5

▶ Transcript of ***Kasage*** Video

Interviewer:	Now let's give you a little more difficult problem that I want you to use the same approach that Julio used, OK? Can you write this problem down for me?
Kasage:	Um hum
Interviewer:	It's six hundred and thirty-eight plus four hundred and seventy-six.
Kasage:	I didn't really get it.
Interviewer:	You didn't get it?
Kasage:	I think it was 34 or something. No, I think it was a thousand something.
Interviewer:	OK, why do you think it was a thousand something?
Kasage:	Because I, those are bigger numbers. They can't add up to 34.
Interviewer:	OK, so can you explain to me what you did here.
Kasage:	Six plus four equals 10, so I put the ten there. And seven plus, seven—seven plus three equals 10, so I put the ten there and I—eight plus 6 equals 14, so I put the 14 there.
Interviewer:	OK. Can you tell me what this 6 represents here?
Kasage:	The hundreds.
Interviewer:	The hundreds? OK, so is that really a six, or is it maybe a bigger number?
Kasage:	It's a bigger number?
Interviewer:	Can you tell me what number it is?

Continued

Kasage:	600?
Interviewer:	600? OK, and what does this four represent here?
Kasage:	400?
Interviewer:	OK, so what would be the answer to this plus this? If this equals 600 and this equals 400. . .
Kasage:	One thousand?
Interviewer:	OK, so would it be ten or would it be the thousand?
Kasage:	Thousand.
Interviewer:	Thousand? OK. Do you maybe want to try working it out that way?
Kasage:	Yeah.
Interviewer:	OK.
Kasage:	Do I still leave the ten and the fourteen there?
Interviewer:	Well, I don't know. Would this be—what does this three represent here?
Kasage:	Tens.
Interviewer:	But what—how many tens?
Kasage:	Thirty.
Interviewer:	Thirty? OK. What does this seven represent here?
Kasage:	Seventy.
Interviewer:	OK, so what would those two numbers add up to?
Kasage:	Ten hundred?
Interviewer:	Ten hundred? Well, we said this was what? What did you say the seven was?
Kasage:	Seventy.
Interviewer:	OK. And what's this one?
Kasage:	Thirty.
Interviewer:	OK, so what are those two numbers added together?
Kasage:	Another one thousand?
Interviewer:	Another one thousand? Really? OK. And what's—this plus that is 14? So do you want to refigure your answer, or do you want to leave it at 34?
Kasage:	I want to redo it.
Interviewer:	Redo it. OK. Did my explaining help you a little bit, or no?
Kasage:	A little bit.
Interviewer:	OK. . . K, so it's 3400. OK.

Source: Philipp, R., Cabral, C., & Schappelle, B. (2011). *Searchable IMAP Video Collection: Children's Mathematical Thinking Clips.* Copyright © 2011 by San Diego State University Research Foundation. All rights reserved except those explicitly licensed to Pearson Education, Inc. Video and transcript were created during IMAP project by Randolph Philipp, Bonnie Schappelle and Candace Cabral.

Step 4:
Complete
the "My
Descriptions"
column of the
worksheet.

Step 5:
Complete
the "My
Interpretations"
column of the
worksheet.

Step 6:
Complete the
rest of the
worksheet.

Step 7:
Reflect on
your work.

Step 4: Complete the "My Descriptions" column of the worksheet. Remember that your goal here is to describe, objectively, things that Kasage does and says that you think are noteworthy and relevant to her understanding of the math.

Step 5: Fill in the "My Interpretations" column of the worksheet. Use the "My Descriptions" column to provide evidence for your interpretations.

Step 6: Complete the rest of the worksheet. See if you can come up with alternative interpretations for Kasage's work. Also note any kinds of questions you'd like to ask Kasage if you had the chance to do so.

Step 7: Reflect on your work. If you are working with others, take a few minutes to share and discuss your descriptions and interpretations. Be sure to support your interpretations with evidence from the video—your notes and worksheet comments will help you do this. Use the study questions to help you reflect on your observations (and, if you are working with others, to start your discussion). You can also use the completed sample worksheet (Table 2.2) to help you think about your own responses and to stimulate your reflections and discussion.

Study Questions

▶ How did you describe Kasage's work? What details did you intentionally leave out of your description?

▶ What evidence did you use in formulating your interpretations?

▶ What alternative interpretations did you make?

▶ What were some strengths and weaknesses you found in Kasage's work?

■ What do you think she understands?

■ What do you think she still needs to work on?

■ If you had been the interviewer, what additional questions would you have liked to ask Kasage?

■ If you were Kasage's teacher, how would you build on her strengths to address those aspects of place value/addition that you think still need work?

Table 2.2   Completed Sample Worksheet: *Kasage* Video

Key Mathematical Ideas:
- Our base-10 number system is built on powers of ten (groupings of 1s, 10s, 100s, 1000s, and so on)
- We can decompose numbers into the values for each place—for example, $638 = 600 + 30 + 8$ and $476 = 400 + 70 + 6$
- We can find partial sums and then add these together to find the sum: $638 + 476 = (600 + 400) + (30 + 70) + (8 + 6)$

My Descriptions	My Interpretations and Supporting Evidence	Alternative Interpretations?	My Questions
Kasage represents the sums of both the "6" and the "4" (in the numbers 600 and 400) and the "7" and the "3" (in the numbers 70 and 30) as 10s, writing both partial sums directly under each other and aligned in the 100s column. 638 +476 10 10 She adds $8 + 6$ and aligns the answer with the other two partial sums, adding them to get 34. 638 +476 10 10 14	She can add the digits ($6 + 4 = 10$ and $7 + 3 = 10$), but she's not clear about the value of these in terms of their "place" in the problem.	She doesn't quite understand Julio's approach, and she's trying to solve the problem his way when it doesn't really make sense to her. She has a somewhat shaky understanding of the place values of the different partial sums but isn't sure about where to put the numbers to capture place value in the written format.	What method would Kasage use to solve the problem on her own? Could she show the value of the digits in the two numbers (638 and 476) with base-10 blocks or some other kind of representation? Is it the notation that's challenging to her? Is the size of the problem she's solving pushing at her level of understanding (i.e., could she solve a smaller problem successfully)?
As Kasage finishes her answer, she says that she thinks it's wrong because it's too small; she estimates that the answer is in the 1000s.	She has—and uses—her number sense to reflect on the reasonableness of her answer.	She hasn't yet fully internalized ideas about place value, and this problem is beyond her current level of comfort in dealing with place value. Since the problem involves adding two three-digit numbers, she figures that the answer will be "big," and saying that a number in the thousands is a way of saying that the sum is likely to be a number that's larger than the ones she typically works with.	Ask her why she thought the sum would be in the thousands.

Continued

	My Interpretations and	Alternative	
My Descriptions	**Supporting Evidence**	**Interpretations?**	**My Questions**
When the interviewer asks her to explain her answer, she says that $6 + 4 = 10$, $7 + 3 = 10$, $8 + 6 = 14$.	She's thinking about adding digits and isn't taking the value of the places into account.	She isn't entirely sure how to add numbers that "cross" a place value boundary. Her understanding is shaky regarding partial sums in a way that consistently captures the place value of the sums.	Is it her understanding of addition of numbers in the 10s, 100s, or 1000s that's a problem, or is her understanding shaky more in terms of *naming* or *writing* the sums? Would she make the same kinds of mistakes if she modeled the problem with base-10 blocks?
Her calculations with addition of single digits are correct. When the interviewer asks her to identify the value of the digits 6 and 4, Kasage correctly identifies them and says that $600 + 400$ is "one thousand."	She knows her basic number facts (sums of numbers less than 10).		Same questions as above.
She begins to correct her work on the problem, changing the "top" partial sum of 10 into 1000. She asks the interviewer whether she should keep the 10 and the 14 from her original solution.	She doesn't have a clear understanding of how to create partial sums to solve this problem.	She has some understanding of how to use partial sums: her difficulty may lie in some combination of computing the partial sums correctly and representing the sums accurately. The size of the numbers she's dealing with seems to be adding to her difficulties.	Same questions as above.
With prompting from the interviewers, Kasage identifies the "3" and the "7" as representing 30 and 70 but isn't sure what their sum is. She says that the sum is 1000 and, despite the interviewer's somewhat incredulous tone, changes the second partial sum (10) to 1000.	While Kasage's observation that 34 is too small an answer suggests that she can reflect on the reasonableness of an answer, she's not applying her number sense here. Kasage is able to understand individual elements of this solution with scaffolding, but her understanding is fragile enough that she's unable to integrate the parts into a sensible approach on her own.	Kasage has given up thinking for herself on this problem and is just trying to get it finished.	Are the interviewer's questions helping Kasage or confusing her further? Would Kasage be able to correctly add 30 and 70 if she weren't feeling obliged to solve this problem Julio's way? Does *she* think she understands Julio's solution process?
She leaves the 14 where it was (written directly under the original 10s) and writes 3400 as her new answer.	Kasage doesn't understand how to notate partial sums in terms of "preserving" groupings in the same columns.	Kasage's answer is in the ballpark of her original prediction (the sum should be "a thousand something"), so she's okay with the solution and happy to be done with the problem.	Is Kasage able to make connections or find correspondences between Julio's solution and other ways of solving the problem? Can she use Julio's way to solve a smaller addition problem (e.g., adding two two-digit numbers)?

Table 2.2   Completed Sample Worksheet: *Kasage* Video

Exercise 5: Myrna

In this final exercise, you will observe Myrna, a second grader, solving a problem about sharing eight brownies among six children. Myrna is an English-language learner, and a translator assists in the interview process.

Process for Viewing and Analyzing the *Myrna* Video. Follow the steps below as you complete the exercise. Read through all the steps before you begin in order to get an overview of the process.

Step 1: **Identify key math ideas.** You will probably want to refer to your work in Exercise 3 for this step given that the problems are virtually identical. Remember, however, that Myrna is a second grader and that the written work from Exercise 3 comes from a fourth-grade class.

Step 2: **Prepare to watch the video.** Make a copy of the blank Chapter 2 worksheet (located in the Appendix and as a writeable PDF on PDToolKit). You may want to read over the transcript before you begin as well (see Figure 2.6); Myrna is not a native English speaker and speaks Spanish with an interpreter during much of the interview, which makes it a bit more difficult to coordinate your viewing of her actions on the video with the conversation. Think about the kind of information you'll need to collect to fill out the worksheet; have some paper on hand for making notes about the details of Myrna's work as you watch the video.

Step 3: **View the *Myrna* clip.** Find the *Myrna* clip on PDToolKit and watch it at least once. Recall that your purpose in viewing the video is to practice describing and interpreting Myrna's work. You may want to view the clip once to get an overall sense of her work and a second (and maybe third) time to gather more detail as you complete your worksheet. Because much of the interaction is in Spanish, as you watch the video you will probably want to look closely at the transcript as well. Keep scratch paper handy to jot down notes and time codes so that you can easily refer back to the evidence you used to build your interpretations.

Step 4: **Complete the "My Descriptions" column of the worksheet.** Remember that your goal here is to describe, objectively, things that Myrna does and says that you think are noteworthy and relevant to her understanding of the math.

Step 5: **Fill in the "My Interpretations" column of the worksheet.** Use the "My Descriptions" column to provide evidence for your interpretations.

Step 6: **Complete the rest of the worksheet.** See if you can come up with alternative interpretations for Myrna's work. Also, note any kinds of questions you'd like to ask her if you had the chance to do so.

Step 1:
Identify key
math ideas.

Step 2:
Prepare to
watch the
video.

Step 3:
View the
Myrna clip.

Step 4:
Complete
the "My
Descriptions"
column of the
worksheet.

Step 5:
Complete
the"My
Interpretations"
column of the
worksheet.

Step 6:
Complete the
rest of the
worksheet.

PDToolkit
for
*Examining Mathematics
Practice through
Classroom Artifacts*

FIGURE 2.6

 Transcript of *Myrna* Video

Interviewer:	If I had eight brownies . . .
Myrna:	Brownies? *What is that?*
Translator:	Brownies? *They're these little cakes . . .*
Myrna:	Oh. Eight?
Interviewer:	And I wanted to share them evenly, okay, with six people. How could I share them?
Translator:	*She wants to share them.*
Myrna:	*How many are there?*
Translator:	*There are eight . . .*
Myrna:	*Eight. And you want to share it, how many?*
Translator:	*To share them with six people. Equally. So that everyone has, the brownies, the same amount.*
Myrna:	*Are there eight? [unintelligible] What was the first number? Of the little cakes?*
Translator:	*Um hum. They're little chocolate cakes.*
Myrna:	*With how many children?*
Translator:	*With six; six people.*
Myrna:	Uh uh. (*Counts under her breath.*) Nhhh.
Translator:	*There are eight and they want to share them equally among six people so each person has the same amount.*
Interviewer:	So is this one brownie?
Myrna:	Uh huh.
Interviewer:	For one child, or one niño?
Interviewer:	Okay. And is this 2, 3, 4, 5, 6? And how many do you have left over?
Myrna:	*(to translator) What?*
Translator:	*How many are left?*

Note: Italic text indicates that the conversation was in Spanish and that the text has been translated.

Continued

Myrna:	Two.
Interviewer:	Two? Okay. So how could you share those with those with these six people? How could you—now these are hard, and they're a block, but a brownie you could cut. Could you cut it somehow?
Translator:	*If you could cut them and share them evenly among everyone, how many would you give them? To each person.*
Myrna:	*How many pieces would you cut?*
Translator:	Um hum
Myrna:	*How many?*
Translator:	Um hum. *Into how many would you cut? . . . six people.*
Myrna:	*In three.*
Interviewer:	*Three?* Three.
Interviewer:	How would you do it?
Myrna:	*(to translator): Tell her I'm going to do it.*
Interviewer:	*How would you do it?*
Myrna:	*How do you say "cut"?*
Interviewer:	"Cut."
Myrna:	Cut . . .
Interviewer:	I'm going to pretend like this is that one brownie that you've got in your hand there. Okay. That's this one. We'll pretend that's this extra one here. And then this is the other brownie that you have in your hand.
Interviewer:	Okay. Now how would you cut those then so that everybody, all the other six, got an equal piece?
Myrna:	Oops! Like this.
Interviewer:	Good job! Very nice.

Source: Philipp, R., Cabral, C., & Schappelle, B. (2011). *Searchable IMAP Video Collection: Children's Mathematical Thinking Clips* Copyright © 2011 by San Diego State University Research Foundation. All rights reserved except those explicitly licensed to Pearson Education, Inc. Video and transcript were created during IMAP project by Randolph Philipp, Bonnie Schappelle and Candace Cabral. Transcript adapted by Lynn Goldsmith and Nahia Kassas.

Step 7: **Reflect on your work.** If you are working with others, take a few minutes to share and discuss your descriptions and interpretations. Be sure to support your interpretations with evidence from the video—your notes and worksheet comments will help you do this. Use the study questions to help you reflect on your observations (and, if you are working with others, to start your discussion). You can also use the completed sample worksheet (Table 2.3) to help you think about your own responses and to stimulate your reflections and discussion.

Study Questions

► How did you describe Myrna's work? What details did you intentionally leave out of your description?

► What evidence did you use in formulating your interpretations?

► What alternative interpretations did you make?

► What were some strengths and weaknesses you found in Myrna's work?

 ▪ What do you think she does and doesn't understand?

 ▪ If you had been the interviewer, what additional questions would you have liked to ask her?

► How do you think language may have figured into Myrna's work?

► What questions does this video raise for you about challenges involved in separating the mathematical demands of tasks from nonmathematical ones? As a teacher, what kinds of accommodations do you make for English-language-learners (or special education students who do not have specific mathematical disabilities) to help them develop mathematically?

TABLE 2.3 Completed Sample Worksheet: *Myrna* Video

Key Mathematical Ideas:
- Division can be thought of as sharing out equal quantities.
- If division results in a "remainder," this remainder can be subdivided in such a way as to share it out equally as well.
- $\frac{1}{3} = \frac{1}{6} + \frac{1}{6}$.

My Descriptions	My Interpretations and Supporting Evidence	Alternative Interpretations?	My Questions
Myrna asks what the first number was as she collects some snap cubes and then checks about the meaning of the word "brownie."	She wants to make sure she understands the problem. This seems to have both a computational component that's related to her collecting the right number of cubes ("what was the first number?") and a linguistic one ("of the little cakes?").	She understands that she's going to have to share out something and, by checking about what a brownie is, may be getting information about how "shareable" it is.	

Continued

TABLE 2.3 Completed Sample Worksheet: *Myrna* Video

My Descriptions	My Interpretations and Supporting Evidence	Alternative Interpretations?	My Questions
She counts out some cubes off-camera and pushes some aside. She counts out six, picks up two cubes that are snapped together, and unsnaps them. She holds one in her left hand and puts the other down. She takes two cubes from the original six. Myrna counts the remaining cubes on the table (she points to six, but they're not all visible in camera), looks briefly at the (three) cubes in her hand, and says "uh huh." She looks a bit puzzled. She recounts, puts one cube back, and looks up at the camera.	She's using the cubes to represent brownies, and she discovers that she has one too many. She's demonstrating "metacognitive" skills, monitoring her work to make sure that she's got the right number of cubes to represent the problem.	She's using the cubes to represent people, and she's gotten confused—perhaps the confusion is about how many cubes she needs or perhaps it's about how representing people will help her solve the problem.	What were you planning on doing? What do these cubes represent?
She pauses, saying "hmmm."	She's not sure what to do to share out the brownies.	She represents the six brownies on the table as being shared among the six children but isn't sure about how to share out the two in her hand.	What do the cubes on the table represent? What do the cubes in your hand represent? Have you shared everything that you can share?
The interpreter repeats the problem—share the brownies out equally. The interviewer points to a cube as the interpreter begins to move away the extra cubes. The interviewer helps move extra cubes, points back at one cube, and asks if it's one child. (Myrna says "yes.") The interviewer touches and counts each cube on the table (getting to six) and asks Myrna how many she has left over.	Myrna agrees with the interviewer that each cube represents a child. But she counted out eight cubes, and there are eight brownies, not eight children, in the problem.	She's not really understanding the interviewer's language, so while she's agreeing that the cube stands for a child, it's not clear what she's agreeing to—the meaning of the representation (cubes = children) or the fact that there are six objects on the table.	Is Myrna thinking about the cubes as children or as brownies? (Back to the questions about what the cubes represent.) Ask her to show how she's representing the children and then separately ask her how she's sharing out the brownies.
The interviewer (with help from the interpreter) asks Myrna how she could cut the remaining two brownies up. Without apparent hesitation, Myrna says she could cut each of the two pieces into three. When asked to draw what she means, she draws each brownie cut into thirds.	She has a strong grasp on how to divide up the remainder and is comfortable thinking about thirds. Instead of dividing each piece into sixths and sharing out a sixth from the first brownie and a sixth from the second, she recognizes that dividing each brownie into thirds will yield one piece for each child.		If there are six children who are sharing the brownies, why did you divide each piece into three? If you had divided each brownie into six pieces, would that have been fair sharing?

47

Seeing the Potential in Students' Thinking

Our parents taught us to learn from our mistakes. We teach our children that mistakes are opportunities to learn. We think of this as commonsense advice. In her book *Mistakes That Worked*, Charlotte Jones lists 40 mistakes that worked—things like ice cream cones, potato chips, sticky notes, penicillin, aspirin, Slinky, Velcro, and doughnut holes. Each of these would not exist without a "mistake." Consider the chocolate chip cookie mistake:

> In 1930, Ruth Wakefield was busy running the Toll House Inn, which is between Boston and New Bedford, Massachusetts. While mixing a batch of cookies, she found out that she was out of baker's chocolate. As a substitute, she broke some sweetened chocolate into small pieces and added them to the cookie dough. She expected the chocolate to melt and the dough to absorb them, making chocolate cookies. When she took out the pan from the oven, she was surprised to see that the chocolate had not melted into the dough, and her cookies were not chocolate cookies. Wakefield had mistakenly invented the chocolate chip cookie. They are named Toll House Cookies after Ruth Wakefield's Inn and are the most popular variety of cookie in America today. (Jones, 1991, p. 6)

We celebrate and are grateful for *these* types of mistakes (especially the yummy ones), and we recognize that they had elements of things that were right. Isn't it interesting that we rarely talk about the mistakes students make in the mathematics classroom in the same manner? In fact, we most often call them errors, and we try to extinguish them as quickly as possible. This view that mistakes are awful and require a rapid corrective action is no surprise given our experiences as mathematics learners and our historical images of how to teach mathematics. School mathematics has been viewed in black-and-white terms—either you are right or you are wrong. In this chapter, we examine the grey area and explore how errors can be useful and productive by turning our focus to consider the potential in students' mistakes.

Why Focus on Errors?

For years, teachers have been taught to remediate and correct errors as quickly as possible in order to avoid confusion (Buswell & Lenore, 1926). Yet more recent research suggests that we can use errors as catalysts for inquiry into student thinking (Borasi, 1987, 1996), as sites for learning, and as opportunities for helping students dig deeper into mathematical concepts (Wearne, Murray, Hiebert et al., 1997). These updated views assume that mistakes can provide insights into the potential in students' thinking. But for teachers to gain the type of skills it takes to look at errors through a new lens—a lens that sees errors as possibilities rather than deficits—they need support.

In this chapter, as in Chapter 2, you will practice describing and interpreting students' mathematical thinking. We'll focus on developing the skills and sensibilities needed to identify and recognize the underlying logic behind students' errors and partial understandings in order to bring you new tools to use in your own practice.

Using Errors to See Potential Instead of Just Deficits in Students' Thinking

Consider the following example:

> Maria, a fourth grader, has been learning about operating with fractions. When asked to add two fractions, her paper shows the following:
> $$\frac{2}{5} + \frac{4}{6} = \frac{6}{11}$$

Maria's error is typical, as any fourth-grade teacher will recognize. But digging beneath the surface may uncover valuable information about the specific difficulties that Maria has encountered in learning fractions and about her understanding of fractions and the rules for operating with fractions. It should be fairly obvious that Maria added the fractions by adding numerators and denominators separately. But we have no information about how she thought about the problem and why she operated on the fractions in the way that she did. There are a variety of possibilities. Maria could have used the rule for multiplying fractions instead of the rule for adding fractions, and she could have done so either *purposefully* (perhaps overgeneralizing about the multiplication rule for all operations involving fractions) or *accidentally* (perhaps by looking quickly at the problem and assuming that it called for multiplication rather than addition). Instead of thinking of each fraction as a single number, Maria might have thought of each as two whole numbers separated by a line. She might then have operated on them using the rules that she knows for adding whole numbers—adding the two "top numbers" and "bottom numbers" separately and then drawing a line between the two "answers" (Borasi, 1987).

Analyzing Maria's work to figure out why she made the mistake is one thing, but we should recognize that this analysis assumes that she didn't know how to perform the operations correctly. We could also ask whether there might be a context in which Maria's thinking could be *right*. Suppose that Maria played on a soccer team and thought about this problem in terms of the tournaments she'd been playing in over the past two consecutive weekends. Imagine that she played five games one weekend and six games the following weekend. The first weekend she won two games, and the second weekend she won four. What if Maria saw $\frac{2}{5} + \frac{4}{6}$ as a ratio problem and thought about it in terms of the relationship between games won and games played? If she did, she could think that she won 6 games out of 11 played, or $\frac{6}{11}$. Maria would be *right* if she had assumed that the two fractions were actually ratios.

Teaching involves more than identifying an incorrect answer (Ball, Thames, & Phelps, 2008). As teachers, quite often we need to be able to figure out the source of the mathematical error in real time (which is very fast paced). But simply seeing answers as wrong doesn't help you figure out what to do to support a student's correct understanding. Error analysis is challenging work, and for too long it has been unrecognized as a substantive part of the work of teaching.

The value of analyzing students' errors lies, in part, in getting a better handle on what students don't yet understand. But analyzing the thinking behind errors and misconceptions is also a powerful way to explore the positive as well—the potential for growth in students' thinking. We've designed the exercises in this chapter to support you in recognizing the potential that student errors provide as springboards for the following:

- Learning about your students' thinking and reasoning
- Supporting your students in gaining conceptual understanding
- Highlighting common misunderstandings and using them for instructional purposes
- Realizing the potential logic in student's errors or misconceptions

This chapter is intended to support you in using a new lens to examine student mistakes. We'll use two classroom video clips from Ms. Spencer's sixth-grade ratio and proportion lesson to practice analyzing errors and looking for potentially correct thinking as students' ideas unfold during the lesson.

As in Chapter 2, you'll practice describing and interpreting students' mathematical thinking through a series of study questions for each exercise. This chapter will hone in on interpreting student errors and examining the ways Ms. Spencer used those errors in her teaching.

Exercise 1: Lemonade Lesson Part 1—Alberto and Kisha

This clip captures part of a class discussion that occurred 26 minutes into Ms. Spencer's lesson on ratio and proportion. Prior to this video clip, Ms. Spencer posed the following problem to her sixth-grade class, writing it on chart paper (see Figure 3.1).

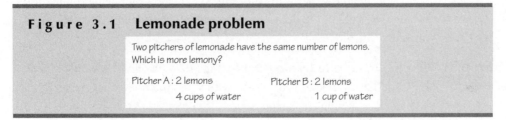

F i g u r e   3 . 1   Lemonade problem

Two pitchers of lemonade have the same number of lemons.
Which is more lemony?

Pitcher A : 2 lemons   Pitcher B : 2 lemons
           4 cups of water   1 cup of water

After some discussion of what "lemony" meant, the students decided that Pitcher B was "more lemony." Ms. Spencer then posed another problem and asked the students to decide whether Alberto's lemonade mixture or Kisha's was more lemony (see Figure 3.2).

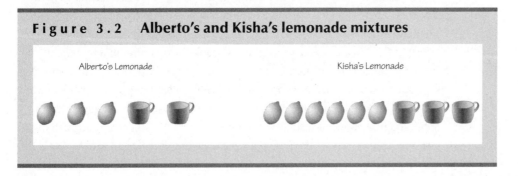

F i g u r e   3 . 2   Alberto's and Kisha's lemonade mixtures

Alberto's Lemonade   Kisha's Lemonade

The students worked on this problem and wrote their conjectures on the chart paper as preparation for class discussion. The video clip begins with Ms. Spencer proposing a conjecture about the relative lemonyness of the two mixtures.

Process for Viewing and Analyzing Lemonade Lesson Part 1. Follow the steps below as you complete this exercise. Read through all the steps before you begin in order to get an overview of the process.

Step 1:
Identify key
math ideas
and skills.

Step 2:
Prepare to
watch the
video.

Step 3:
View the
*Lemonade
Lesson #1*
clip.

Step 1: Identify key math ideas and skills. Before you watch the video, carefully examine the math task that students are working on and make sure that you understand it. Answer the following questions for yourself:

- Which pitcher of lemonade is more lemony? Why?
- What are the key mathematical ideas and skills this problem taps?
- What do you predict students will answer? Why?
- What misconceptions or errors might students have when solving this problem?
- How do you think the teacher is interpreting the student's understanding? What might be her evidence?

Step 2: Prepare to watch the video. Make a copy of the blank Chapter 3 worksheet (see Figure 3.3; a blank worksheet is located in the Appendix and as a writeable PDF on PDToolKit). Also have some paper on hand for making notes about the details of the students' comments and actions as you watch the video.

PDToolkit
for
*Examining Mathematics
Practice through
Classroom Artifacts*

Step 3: View the *Lemonade Lesson #1* clip. Find the *Lemonade Lesson #1* clip on PDToolKit. Although you worked with video interviews in Chapter 2, viewing classroom video can be a very different experience. It's often difficult to focus on only a few aspects of the class, particularly if the room layout, students, equipment, grade level, or other aspects of the class look or feel very different from your own teaching context. We suggest that you watch the entire clip first just to get familiar with the classroom, teacher, and students. Then view it a second time to complete the exercise.

Remember that you are viewing the video in order to describe and interpret the errors students make and to look for potential mathematical strengths in their reasoning. Use the columns on the worksheet as a focus for your viewing. Since the clip is nearly 10 minutes long, you might want to pause the video when you encounter an error and use your notepaper to jot down the time code as well as the details of what the students (and perhaps also the teacher) say or do. One strength of using video as an artifact is

Figure 3.3   **Blank Chapter 3 worksheet**

Chapter 3 Worksheet: Examining Errors and Misconceptions

Key Mathematical Ideas:

Error or Misconception	Potential (what the student knows)	New Insights and/or Curiosities

that you can stop, pause, and replay it if you want to revisit something that someone did or said. This ability to replay and revisit can help a lot in your analysis of students' thinking.

Step 4: **Complete the "Error or Misconception" column of the worksheet.** Write down the errors you notice and also note any conjectures you have about the thinking behind them—why do you think students made the errors they did? Try to be as specific as possible. You may want to fill in this part of the worksheet while viewing the video or perhaps after you have seen the whole clip—do whatever works best for you.

Step 5: **Complete the "Potential" column of the worksheet.** Write down descriptions of what students do seem to know and/or your conjectures about the possible logic of their thinking.

Step 6: **Complete the "New Insights and/or Curiosities" column of the worksheet.** You may not initially have a lot to write down in terms of new insights or things you're curious about. But getting in the habit of asking yourself what's interesting or puzzling about students' work and being open to new insights about students' thinking is an important step in taking a deeper look at how instruction works with students' understanding, so we encourage you to take some time with this column.

Step 7: **Reflect on your work.** If you are working with others, take a few minutes to share and discuss your descriptions and interpretations. Be sure to support your interpretations with evidence from the video—your notes and worksheet

Step 4: Complete the "Error or Misconception" column of the worksheet.

Step 5: Complete the "Potential" column of the worksheet.

Step 6: Complete the "New Insights and/or Curiosities" column of the worksheet.

Step 7: Reflect on your work.

comments will help you do this. You might want to look over the completed sample worksheet to help you think about your own responses. Use the study questions as well to help you reflect on your observations (and, if you are working with others, to start your discussion).

Study Questions

► How would you describe the errors students were making?

► What about their thinking was on the right track?

► What potential rationale could you imagine they had for their thinking?

► What could be the teacher's purpose in posing an incorrect conjecture? How might this help students understand the concept better?

TABLE 3.1 Completed Sample Worksheet: Lemonade Lesson Part 1

Key Mathematical Ideas:
- This is a problem that requires thinking proportionally, not additively.
- Because the relationship between quantities is critical, students have to think about the two amounts in a coordinated way.

Error or Misconception	Potential (what the student knows)	New Insights and/or Curiosities
Alberto's is more lemony because it has less water.	Pitcher B was more lemony, and it had less water; therefore, Alberto's is more lemony because it has less water. • Reasoning by analogy (from results of Pitcher B to Alberto's lemonade) • Recognition that amount of water influences lemonyness	The teacher's purposeful use of students' previous comments about Pitcher B to potentially cause disequilibrium that would encourage students to evaluate the *relationship* between water and lemons (Alberto's has less water, but Kisha's is more lemony).
Jose: Kisha's is more lemony because it has a lot of lemons.	Jose could be interpreting "lemony" as "has more lemons" or "a lot of lemons" without thinking about the amount of water in the pitcher.	The teacher seems to anticipate this error and uses the example of Pitchers E and F to challenge this way of thinking. (Pitcher E has more lemons, but it is not more lemony.)
Kenny: Kisha's "has more."	Kenny could be answering the question "which one has more lemonade?" rather than the question the teacher posed ("which one is more lemony?").	Even when you *think* the task is clear, students might be interpreting it differently and answering a different question. It's important to check errors to see whether this might be the case.

Commentary on Lemonade Lesson Part 1. A central mathematical idea that students are confronting in this lesson is that proportional reasoning involves coordinating the relationship between quantities instead of simply attending to increases or decreases in a single quantity. We see the following aspects of the video clip as salient in terms of student errors and the teacher's use of errors as the lesson unfolds:

- Ms. Spencer posed a common student misconception as her own conjecture to see if others agreed with it—Alberto's is more lemony because it has less water. She explicitly related her conjecture to the previous problem that launched the lesson—pitcher B was more lemony because the students said "it had less water."

- Many students were focused on one aspect—lemons or water but not the *relationship* between the two.

  - Some students had the right answer (Kisha's is more lemony) but used incomplete reasoning. They attended to only one of the two components of the mixture and seemed to be thinking additively, for example, arguing that "it's more lemony because it has more lemons."

  - Some students used the same kind of incomplete reasoning but got an incorrect answer (Alberto's is more lemony)—"it's more lemony because it had less water."

CCSS—Grade 6
Understand ratio concepts and use ratio reasoning to solve problems. p. 42.

CCSS–Mathematical Practices
Reason abstractly and quantitatively. p. 6.
Make sense of problems and persevere in solving them. p. 6.

- Because Ms. Spencer had predicted before the lesson started that students would make errors that focused on comparing amounts of water or number of lemons (but not the *proportion* of lemon to water), she had prepared a poster with problems that would challenge students' thinking (see Figure 3.4).

For Pitchers E and F, she asked two questions:

- Which one is more lemony?
- Which one has more lemons?

Figure 3.4   Ms. Spencer's challenge problem

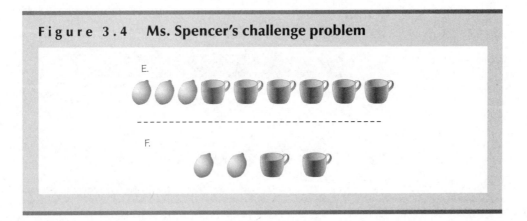

This contrast challenges the idea that the number of lemons determines the lemonyness since the pitcher with more lemons is *not* the most lemony.

Reflecting on Exercise 1. Take a few minutes to reflect on this exercise:

- Were you able to notice the errors (or partial errors) that students made while reasoning about the problem?
- How was what you noticed similar and different from what we noticed?
- Did you find things that we didn't take note of?
- Were you surprised by anything?

Exercise 2: Lemonade Lesson Part 2—Rosa and Maria

Exercise 2 offers more practice examining, describing, and interpreting students' errors. This clip captures students' work a little further on in Ms. Spencer's lemonade lesson. Prior to this clip, Ms. Spencer asked the students whether the lemonade in Pitcher C or Pitcher D was more lemony (see Figure 3.5).

A discussion ensued among the class as students examined the relationship between water and lemons in these two pitchers. The students decided that Pitcher C was more lemony even though Pitcher D had less water. Ms. Spencer returned to Alberto and Kisha's charts to show a pairing of one lemon and one cup of water (Kisha has two lemons per cup; Alberto has one and a half per cup). The students decide that Kisha's was more lemony.

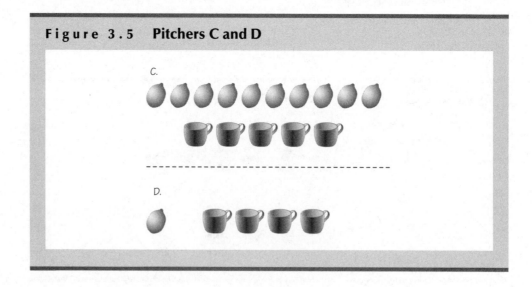

Figure 3.5   Pitchers C and D

C.

D.

Ms. Spencer asked her students if they thought they had a strategy for solving these kinds of problems all the time and then posed a new problem:

> Rosa's pitcher has six lemons/two cups of water, and Maria's pitcher has three lemons/one cup of water.

She asked the students to solve the problem individually and then to discuss their solutions with partners. Video clip 2 captures the whole-class discussion that follows the partner conversations.

Process for Viewing and Analyzing Lemonade Lesson Part 2. Your process for viewing and analyzing the video clip will be similar to the one you used in the first exercise. In this exercise, we'll explore students' reasoning a bit further.

Step 1: Familiarize yourself with the new problem. Make some predictions about how you think students will approach it. What might they say? What errors might they make? What might the reasoning be behind their errors?

Step 2: Prepare to watch the video. Make another copy of the blank Chapter 3 worksheet (in the Appendix and as a writeable PDF on PDToolKit) and get some more scratch paper in case you want to make notes about what you observe. Be sure to include time codes so that you can refer back to parts of the video that are noteworthy.

Step 3: View the *Lemonade Lesson #2* clip. Find the *Lemonade Lesson #2* clip on PDToolKit. Remember that your purpose in viewing the video is to describe and interpret students' errors and also to see how those errors might contain the seeds of more developed thinking.

Step 4: Fill out the blank worksheet. You may want to view the video clip a second time as you complete the worksheet:

- Fill in the "Error or Misconception" column, noting errors you observe and making conjectures about the thinking behind them. Try to be as specific as possible. Stop the video when you notice an error if it helps you to record more accurately.

- Fill in the "Potential" column with a description of what the student knows or how his or her reasoning provides a window into plausible thinking.

- Fill in the "New Insights and/or Curiosities" column with anything new you may be thinking about.

Step 1: Familiarize yourself with the new problem.

Step 2: Prepare to watch the video.

Step 3: View the *Lemonade Lesson #2* clip.

Step 4: Fill out the blank worksheet.

Step 5:
Analyze the relationship between the "Error or Misconception" and "Potential" columns.

Step 6:
Reflect on your work.

Step 5: **Analyze the relationship between the "Error or Misconception" and "Potential" columns.** How do you see the understandings that students do have relating to the errors you observed? How might the context of making lemonade potentially influence their thinking? How does Ms. Spencer use students' errors to challenge their thinking and, it is hoped, help them reason correctly about the proportions of water and lemons?

Step 6: **Reflect on your work.** If you are working with others, take a few minutes to share and discuss your descriptions and interpretations. Be sure to support your interpretations with evidence from the video—your notes and worksheet comments will help you do this. The study questions below and the completed sample worksheet (see Table 3.2) can also help you reflect on your observations (and, if you are working with others, to start your discussion).

Study Questions

▶ What errors (or partial errors) did you notice students making as they reasoned about the problem?

▶ How was what you noticed similar and different from what we noticed? Did you find things that we didn't take note of?

▶ Were you surprised by anything you saw in the video?

▶ If you were these students' teacher, what questions might you ask them? What might you do next? What would you hope to achieve as the result of your actions?

Commentary on Lemonade Lesson Part 2. In this video clip, students continued to grapple with the role that lemons and water play in determining lemonyness. We noticed a couple of specific teacher actions in relationship to students' conceptions and misunderstandings about ratio:

- As in the first clip, Ms. Spencer again used purposeful examples to help students attend to more than one aspect of the lemon/water mixture. At the end of the clip, Markisha does focus on the relationship between the lemons and water when she talks about "watered-down lemonade."

- Ms. Spencer also challenges the idea that the amount of water determines lemonyness by contrasting Pitchers C and D. In this case, the pitcher with the least amount of water is not more lemony, and students are challenged to think about the meaning of this counterexample.

Key Mathematical Ideas (same as Part 1):

- This is a problem that requires thinking proportionally, not additively.
- Because the relationship between quantities is critical, students have to think about the two amounts in a coordinated way.

Error or Misconception	Potential (what the student knows)	New Insights and/or Curiosities
Rosa's is more lemony. Students might be paying attention to the total amount of liquid: more liquid means greater lemonyness.	Rosa's has more lemonade; therefore, it is more lemony.	Again, this raises the importance of clarity of questions; many students appear to be answering the question "Which one has more lemonade?" rather than "Which one is more lemony?"
Maria's is more lemony. Students might be paying attention to the total amount of liquid: less liquid means greater concentration of lemon.	Maria's has less lemonade, so it is stronger (more lemony).	Definition of lemony may not be shared among the students.

Reflecting on Exercise 2. Take a couple of minutes to reflect on this exercise: were you able to notice the errors (or partial errors) that students made while reasoning about the lemonade problems? How was what you noticed similar and different from what we noticed? Did you find things that we didn't mention? Were you surprised by anything? Did viewing the second video clip provide additional insights into the first video clip? If so, how? What questions do the two video clips together raise for you?

General Commentary About Errors

As far back as 1987, Raffaella Borasi highlighted the opportunity that errors can provide in the exploration of mathematics. Errors can be valuable sources of information about students' misconceptions. Indeed, the realization that errors can be valuable is well known in the computer programming industry. Debugging isn't just about finding "silly" errors or omissions; it also involves getting clearer about what it takes to actually get things right. By seeing how something doesn't work, you can understand more about how to correct the problem. We're not arguing that all errors lead to stimulating mathematical inquiry, but we do think that they can be useful both as ways to diagnose students' current understanding and as teaching aids in the classroom. Being on the lookout for common errors and asking questions like "what makes sense about this error?" or "in what situations would this reasoning work?" can help provide additional insights into students' thinking. And these insights, in turn, can help guide your instructional decisions.

Dealing with students' errors is part of the everyday work of teachers. This work often requires you to do the following:

- Recognize quickly whether an answer is correct

- Probe students for the reasoning behind their answers (both correct and incorrect ones)

- Figure out if the reasoning behind an error makes sense in some way—for example, whether a student is using reasoning from another situation and generalizing (incorrectly) to the current one or whether the answer is to a different question than the one you thought you were asking

- Figure out if the reasoning behind a *correct* answer actually reflects erroneous thinking

- Predict typical or common misconceptions or errors and plan instruction around them (or plan to highlight them) in order to help students develop conceptual understanding

Working with Errors in Your Own Practice

As you think about your own experience with students' errors, consider the following questions. Discuss your thoughts with your colleagues.

- What kinds of errors do your students repeatedly make in particular content areas? What could the reasoning behind these common errors be? In what situations might their errors make sense?

- How do you take advantage of errors as opportunities for your students to learn? Do students in your class see them as a normal part of the process of making sense of mathematics?

- Are students comfortable making errors and/or talking about errors in ways that are productive, or do they treat errors as embarrassing and avoid examining them?

We conclude this chapter by returning to ways you might use common classroom artifacts and practices from your own classroom to focus on the potential that student errors offer for productive mathematical learning.

Homework

Homework can provide a great window into the errors that students make while solving problems. You can also use homework to get a sense of the types of errors that your class, as a whole, is making. As in Ms. Spencer's class, perhaps your students make a few predictable errors in their thinking about particular mathematical content. Or they might show errors that are different from the ones that you expect. When you review students' homework, ask yourself what the errors your students make can tell you about how they're thinking about the problem. In what ways do their errors make sense? In what ways might you use their errors to stimulate learning opportunities?

Warm-Ups

As with homework, class warm-ups are an opportunity to elicit common misunderstandings. Since warm-ups are often 10 to 15 minutes in length, you might consider using them sometimes to do a quick check on the kinds of errors students are making. Additionally, you may want to show a common error and ask students to analyze it—can *they* determine where the faulty reasoning is and how it can be corrected?

Class Discussions

Problems posed as part of lessons, homework, or warm-ups can all serve to help fuel a class discussion in which errors and mistakes can be used as means for examining underlying mathematical ideas.

Periodic Diagnostic Interviews

Many mathematics educators advocate interviewing students periodically as a way of getting a fuller picture of their mathematical thinking (Burns, 2010; van de Walle, 2004). A diagnostic interview is a one-on-one discussion with a student that's designed to help you gain insight into his or her content understanding and problem-solving processes.

The teacher can use these girls' different block representations to get a sense of how they understand multiplication.

(The interviews you observed in Chapter 2 are examples of diagnostic interviews.) These interviews can be short and targeted, lasting 5 to 10 minutes, or longer and more exploratory—some diagnostic interviews can last as long as half an hour. You may want to conduct diagnostic interviews with students whose errors are puzzling to you in order to try to get a better handle on how they are thinking. These interviews can be done while other students are working independently or after school.

Wrapping Up

This chapter offered you a chance to grind and polish your "student error" lens, using it to look at errors as learning (and teaching) opportunities rather than as embarrassments or signs of mathematical inability. This kind of investigation of student errors requires the descriptive and interpretive lenses that we used in Chapter 2, and also the disposition to suspend taking an evaluative stance toward students' work in favor of assuming a more curious and inquiring attitude. We may all agree that a student's response is incorrect, but we probably also want to be cautious about rushing to an interpretation based solely on what he or she can't do and doesn't understand. Instead, we want to consider the strengths that might be hidden in the erroneous or underdeveloped thinking—strengths that might provide a toehold for our further instructional efforts.

Section 2
Attention to Content

Skillful Use of Artifacts Framework	
SKILLFUL USE OF ARTIFACTS INVOLVES:	
Attention to Thinking	**Attention to Content**
▶ distinguish between description and interpretation of work represented in artifacts	▶ use a guiding mathematical framework to discuss the mathematical content in artifacts
▶ ground interpretations of thinking in evidence from artifacts	▶ compare/contrast different representations of mathematical ideas captured in artifacts
▶ generate plausible alternative interpretations of thinking and justify ideas with evidence	▶ compare/contrast mathematical explanations and solution methods represented in artifacts
▶ see strengths (not just weaknesses) in thinking and understanding captured in artifacts	▶ use the exploration of mathematics to develop/engage norms of mathematical argument

Source: Adapted from Nikula, J., Goldsmith, L. T., Blasi, Z. V., & Seago, N. (2006). A framework for the strategic use of classroom artifacts in mathematics professional development. *NCSM Journal, 9*(1), 59.

In this section, we consider the right-hand column of the Skillful Use of Artifacts framework, turning our attention to the *mathematical content* of the activities that generate students' thinking. By analyzing the kind of mathematics we ask our students to do we can be more purposeful in providing rigorous mathematical experiences. We can also better anticipate and facilitate students' negotiation of the content by understanding the mathematical demands of the tasks themselves.

The ways we use classroom artifacts—and even the kinds of artifacts we use will be different in this section. In Section 1, we focused on artifacts where students were at the center. We worked with written work and video to get a purchase on students' thinking and on the ways that teachers worked with students' ideas. In Section 2, we'll treat curriculum materials as classroom artifacts, using them to investigate how their mathematical content might affect students' opportunities to learn.

Chapter 4 explores two guiding mathematical frameworks that can help us recognize and promote rigorous thinking by directing our focus to the relevant mathematics underlying students' work. These frameworks are useful for planning and implementing lessons that address impor-

tant mathematical ideas and skills, for shaping our responses to students' ideas during class in ways that keep the mathematical work worthwhile and challenging, and for reviewing and analyzing students' work after class in order to plan subsequent lessons.

Chapter 5 considers different mathematical representations and explanations in the context of a single problem. The importance of using representations to model and describe mathematical situations runs throughout the groundbreaking policy documents of the National Council of Teachers of Mathematics and figures heavily in the Common Core Standards. In this chapter, we consider how different representations of a problem solution relate to one another and how they can emphasize different mathematical aspects of the same problem.

In both Chapters 4 and 5, the focus is on analyzing the mathematical ideas that students encounter in their work. Examining these ideas should position you better to help students develop their mathematical understanding, make conceptual connections, and develop the depth and flexibility of thinking that comes from being able to approach a problem from different perspectives.

Keeping an Eye on Rigorous Mathematics: Big Ideas and Habits of Mind

A group of second-grade teachers who had been piloting new curriculum materials sat down together after school to discuss how it was going. Most were having very positive experiences, but Jasmine had some concerns she wanted to raise with the group. "I don't know," she mused. "This program jumps all over the place, and it's really confusing my kids!" She got out her textbook and shuffled pages until she found a chapter on addition. "Look at this! We're doing the number line, and then the next day I'm teaching time! And two days later, it's a money lesson. How can the kids possibly keep things straight when things are all over the place?"

Nguyet, another second-grade teacher, said that she saw things differently. "I agree that the contexts skip around, but I guess I'd been thinking about this chapter as giving kids different ways to think about adding. In each of those lessons, kids add in chunks of five. They jump five on the number line and add nickels and add five-minute increments on the clock. So I haven't been so worried about whether kids can recognize nickels or tell time. Instead, I've been focusing on different ways to model adding fives."

In this conversation, Jasmine and Nguyet seem to be reading the same lessons from different angles. While Nguyet is looking for the mathematical threads that hold the whole chapter together, Jasmine is looking at a more molecular level at the activities that make up a lesson. Jasmine's orientation is important for ensuring that lessons go smoothly, but without a perspective like Nguyet's, students are likely to experience their lessons as a collection of disjointed and disconnected activities—which is how Jasmine herself described them.

In this chapter, we'll use a mathematical framework that will help to focus on the conceptual underpinnings of your curriculum—the "big ideas" driving students' work over the year. These big ideas help to create coherence and connections among the activities that make up individual lessons and curriculum units. And while this particular chapter zeroes in on attending to big ideas, we've already done work with them in this book. Recall that in Chapter 2 we based our interpretations of student work in terms of key mathematical ideas involved in the problems students solved, and in Chapter 3 we considered students' errors in light of core ideas. In this chapter, we'll extend that work by identifying how big ideas play out over a whole unit of study and also within a lesson. The classroom artifacts we analyze in this chapter include curriculum materials themselves.

When you analyze your curriculum materials in terms of their conceptual arc and the intellectual demands they make on students, you're honing in on the parts of the math program that are most consequential for students' developing rigorous and flexible mathematical understanding. The more you're able to analyze the program in terms of the big mathematical ideas, the more you'll be prepared to identify mathematically important elements in curriculum units, chapters, and lessons—and to emphasize the ideas and their interconnections as you work with students.

Naming and Framing Mathematical Rigor

Before the current round of math education reform, a mathematically rigorous education was generally considered to be one that required students to apply their knowledge of facts and procedures to increasingly complex and numerically challenging problems—and to do so efficiently and accurately. The emphasis on facts and procedures wasn't all that much different from views of rigor in other subject matter areas. If you're of a certain age, you probably remember grammar lessons dedicated to identifying parts of speech and diagramming alarmingly complex sentences, social studies assignments that required using encyclopedias to do reports about the economy and geography of different countries (we often tried to spiff them up with drawings of the countries' flags), or memorizing the parts of the different body systems in science.

Beginning in the late 1980s with the National Council of Teachers of Mathematics (NCTM) *Standards*, educators reframed expectations for math teaching and learning (NCTM, 1989, 1991). Along with these changes came a reconsideration of what constituted a mathematically rigorous education. As a field, we've moved away from an emphasis on rote learning in favor of developing students' mathematical reasoning and sense making. Today, mathematical rigor is at least as much about promoting effective mathematical thinking as it is about the ability to use procedures to solve computationally complex but routine problems. Although no one would deny that there's an important role for accurate and efficient computational ability in a rigorous mathematical education, we've also come to recognize the central importance of promoting students' ability to think like mathematicians. Rigorous mathematical thinking involves both command of the content and being able to explore and reason about novel or complex mathematical situations.

This reconceptualization of what counts as important mathematical knowledge and skill has led to the need to revisit the frameworks we use to understand the goals and purposes of instructional materials. Historically, both textbook authors and teachers have framed math curriculum and instruction in terms of discrete topics—for example, addition and subtraction of single-digit numbers, graphing, addition and subtraction of multidigit numbers, fractions, and geometry. In the sections that follow, we propose two alternative mathematical frameworks to guide our exploration of mathematical tasks: (1) big ideas—the key mathematical concepts that underlie particular content and (2) the mathematical processes and habits of mind that are involved in mathematical work—these are what the NCTM *Principles and Standards* referred to as mathematical processes and the Common Core State Standards (CCSS) describe as mathematical practices.

These frameworks are useful for keeping the important mathematics at the forefront of lesson planning and implementation and for focusing our attention to and analysis of students' thinking. Guiding frameworks help us to plan lessons that address important mathematical ideas and skills, respond to students during class in ways that keep the mathematics worthwhile and challenging, focus our analysis of classroom artifacts, and provide students with a more coherent, connected set of mathematical experiences.

Mathematical Frameworks: Big Ideas and Habits of Mind

Every subject area discipline has its own set of centrally important ideas and ways of thinking. These are the particular ideas and skills that are foundational for building deep and lasting knowledge, the discipline-specific criteria for argumentation and proof, and special vocabulary and modes of discourse. The expert's command of the central concepts and fluency with disciplinary ways of thinking and communicating may seem foreign to the uninitiated. (For example, just think about what it's like to try to understand the terms and conditions of your credit card.) Central ideas and ways of thinking form the core of disciplinary knowledge. In the case of K–12 mathematics, educators talk about *big ideas*—central mathematics concepts—and *mathematical practices* and *habits of mind*—ways of thinking particular to math (CCSS, 2010; Cuoco, Goldenberg, & Mark, 1996; Goldsmith, Mark, & Kantrov, 2000; NCTM, 2000; Schifter, 1996; Schifter & Fosnot, 1993). The major goal of mathematics education is to promote students' learning with respect to these two broad areas, as they are requisite elements for thinking deeply and flexibly about mathematical situations and problems. For this reason, our own work and the work of others rely on mathematical frameworks that are built around one or both of these two core aspects of mathematics understanding and skill.

Big Ideas. Big ideas form the conceptual fabric of mathematics. Deborah Schifter and Catherine Fosnot describe big ideas as "principles that define mathematical order" (Schifter & Fosnot, 1993, p. 35). They are the foundational ideas from which we build further mathematical knowledge and skill. For example, Schifter and Fosnot observe that one big idea for elementary students is that we can count groups of objects as well as single objects themselves. This idea is fundamental to an understanding of place value and also multiplication and division.

Big ideas are not the same as the mathematical topics that often provide the organization of textbooks. Many texts, particularly more traditional ones, title units or chapters with names of topics, for example, *linear algebra*, *fractions*, or *multiplication*, and identify individual lessons in terms of subtopics or skills, such as *using tables to identify equations*, *adding fractions with unlike denominators*, or *multidigit multiplication*. While mathematical topics are important, they don't necessarily organize mathematical study in a coherent way. Without a set of principles to provide the conceptual order that Schifter and Fosnot emphasize, it's easy for students to see math as simply a laundry list of disparate and disconnected facts and procedures to memorize, missing the idea that math can (and *should*) have an internal logic and consistency.

Many textbooks, for example, treat addition and subtraction as separate topics in separate chapters. This separation deemphasizes their connection as inverse operations. Yet this arithmetic property of inverseness is fundamental to successfully solving computation problems and to thinking algebraically as well. The tendency for textbooks (and therefore teachers) to treat addition and subtraction as distinct operations probably lies behind some teachers' surprise that young children often report using addition to solve problems that adults see as calling for subtraction.

For example, consider the "seashells" problem:

> Jim and his brother Alan collected seashells at the beach. Alan found 20. Jim found 12. How many more seashells did Alan find than Jim found?

Did you think about solving this problem by using subtraction to compare the two quantities: $20 - 12 = 8$? As you know, many primary school students would instead treat it as an addition problem, counting up from 12 to 20 and keeping track of the size of the count to find the difference.

Let's consider one more example of a math topic that also relates to inverse operations, one that we'll return to later in this chapter. Most elementary-level textbooks include lessons about "fact families." Often, teachers think about these lessons as opportunities to improve students' computational fluency (which they undoubtedly are). However, as we'll see in Exercise 2, there are also important conceptual reasons

---

Identifying Big Ideas

References to "big ideas" are common both in the research literature and in writings for practitioners. Policy documents such as the CCSS and NCTM *Principles and Standards* call on big ideas in their identification of important mathematical knowledge and skill. In their *Developing Mathematical Ideas* series, Deborah Schifter, Virginia Bastable, Susan Jo Russell, and their colleagues have articulated many of the big ideas that form the conceptual underpinnings of elementary and middle school mathematics. Below are some of the themes they identify related to number and operation:

- Strategies for multidigit computation rely on the base-10 structure of the number system and the properties of the operations.
- The value of a number is determined by multiplying the value of each digit by the value of the place and then summing. For all whole numbers, the value of the place farthest to the right is 1; the value of every other place is 10 times the value of the place to its right.
- The same situation can be represented by an addition and a subtraction sentence.
- A study of the result of multiplying any number by 10 reveals aspects of the base-10 structure of the number system.
- Numbers between 0 and 1 can be expressed using an extension of the whole number place value system.
- The same situation can be represented by a multiplication and a division sentence.
- The same basic principles that govern operations with whole numbers are called upon to operate with fractions or mixed numbers, but the interpretation of each operation may need to be expanded.
- The same quantity can be represented by different fraction names depending on what is taken as 1, the unit or the whole.
- The value of a fraction is determined by the relationship between the numerator and the denominator.

Source: List adapted from Schifter, Bastable, and Russell (2010a, pp. 15, 59, 217; 2010b, pp. 15, 87, 235).

for exposing students to such sets of related computations—reasons that, when made explicit, students can internalize and use in the future to help them figure out new and unfamiliar problems.

There are compelling reasons, therefore, to apply a big ideas framework to both curriculum and instruction. We also see it as a useful and important framework for analyzing the mathematical content of classroom artifacts.

Habits of Mind. A second framework focuses on mathematical practices and habits of mind. The CCSS emphasizes eight mathematical practices that reflect ways of working mathematically; habits of mind similarly refer to ways of thinking that are fundamental to mathematics as a discipline (Cuoco, Goldenberg, & Mark, 1996, 2010; Driscoll, 1999, 2007). "Habits" and "practices" are closely interconnected. Both highlight ways of thinking and working that have become second nature to those steeped in mathematical study (Table 4.1). For example, both emphasize the simple but powerful focus on making sense of mathematical problems and situations. Though this emphasis on sense making is at least as old as the NCTM *Standards* documents from the early 1990s (NCTM, 1989, 1991), math instruction still doesn't always focus on cultivating students' sense of resourcefulness and belief that they can rely on their own knowledge and reasoning to understand the mathematics they study. In fact, we're sometimes struck when we still hear teachers talking about math "magic" or "tricks" with their students rather than encouraging them to think about how or why particular solutions or procedures work as they do.

TABLE 4.1 Mathematical Practices and Habits of Mind

Mathematical Practices	Mathematical Habits of Mind
• Make sense of problems and persevere in solving them.	• Expect math to make sense
• Reason abstractly and quantitatively.	• Observe and describe
• Construct viable arguments and critique the reasoning of others.	• Create and use representations
• Model with mathematics.	• Generalize from examples
• Use appropriate tools strategically.	• Perform thought experiments
• Attend to precision.	• Make conjectures and conduct "real" experiments
• Look for and make use of structure.	• Adopt multiple points of view
• Look for and express regularity in repeated reasoning.	• Ask "why does this work?"
	• Find, describe, and explain patterns
	• Work backward as well as forward
	• Think about simpler cases
	• Reason using relationships
	• Think about extreme cases
	• Justify and defend claims

Source: CCSS (2010)   *Source:* After Cuoco et al. (1996, 2010).

As students develop the disposition to make sense of the math they study, they are better able to develop coherent conceptual understanding, use that understanding to help them think through solutions to novel or unfamiliar problems, and monitor their work for reasonableness. The mathematical practices/habits of mind framework provides us with a tool to analyze student thinking in terms of how students are internalizing the dispositions and processes that help to keep mathematical problem solving and inquiry moving in productive directions.

Mathematical Practices and Habits of Mind

Why do we want to develop students' mathematical practices and habits of mind? We're not expecting every student we teach to go on to have stellar careers as mathematicians, so why do we care whether they think like mathematicians? A large part of the answer lies in the leverage these practices and habits provide when we're faced with new and unfamiliar (nonroutine) mathematical tasks. In these conditions, well-developed mathematical practices and deeply ingrained habits of mind help us to make connections to ideas and situations we *do* understand and to represent, reason, and reflect on our thinking in productive ways.

The mathematical practices recently articulated by the CCSS share much in common with the habits of mind that mathematics educators have emphasized for more than a decade. Some of the examples of habits of mind correspond quite closely to elements of mathematical practice—for example, the emphasis on sense making, using representations, and attending to patterns and regularities.

Other habits of mind unpack some of the aspects of practice. The CCSS mathematical practices identify the propensity to seek and use structure as a core mathematical practice; we might ask what this practice might look like "in the field." Chances are that it involves a variety of habits of mind, including asking why something works, looking for invariants, generalizing from examples, looking for regularities in repeated calculations, and reasoning about relationships.

Habits of mind might remind you of problem-solving strategies commonly featured in math textbooks, such as *guess and check, make an organized list, draw a diagram, make a table*, or *act it out*. Students who have developed mathematical habits of mind are likely to call on these kinds of strategies (and others) to solve problems, but habits of mind are not simply a laundry list that students are taught to follow. Al Cuoco, Paul Goldenberg, and June Mark describe the potential pitfall of thinking about habits of mind as particular problem-solving strategies in this way:

When asked to describe mathematics, they [students] should be able to say something like, "it's about ways for solving problems" instead of "it's about triangles" or "solving equations" or "doing percent." The danger of wishing for this is that it is all too easy to turn "It's about ways for solving problems" into a curriculum that drills students in the five steps for solving a problem. This is not what we are after; we are after mental habits that allow students to develop a repertoire of general heuristics and approaches that can be applied in many different situations. (Cuoco et al., 1996, p. 378)

Choosing and Using a Mathematical Framework for Analyzing Artifacts

You can learn a lot about students' mathematical thinking when you analyze their work using either a big ideas or a practices/habits of mind framework. The big ideas framing will help you focus on the conceptual understanding that is so important for building a solid mathematical foundation; the practices/habits of mind framework will help you examine students' development of the disciplinary ways of thinking that promote robust and productive approaches to mathematical work. These frameworks also provide useful lenses for analyzing mathematics tasks themselves and for helping address the question of whether we're asking students to undertake work that has the potential to engage them in significant and satisfying mathematical learning. Whether you choose a big ideas framework or a practices/habits of mind one will depend on your particular goals at a particular moment. Either will help sharpen your focus on consequential aspects of the mathematics.

You may, in fact, want to use both frameworks in order to build a full picture of the mathematical thinking involved in a given task or problem. (To this end, we've included questions related to both frameworks in our exercises.) If you do, we recommend that at first you make two passes through the work, analyzing it for big ideas in one pass and mathematical practices/habits of mind in another. This way, you'll be able to keep your focus sharp and avoid attending to too much at one time. As we noted earlier, we're working with a different kind of classroom artifact in this chapter—curriculum materials rather than student work itself.

Exercise 1: Identifying Big Ideas in Your Math Textbook

For most teachers, the tasks and activities they use in class come from district-mandated curriculum materials and perhaps also from supplementary materials that they find themselves. The mathematical framing that organizes these materials may not be explicitly articulated to the user. Some textbooks, for example, are framed in terms of topic-by-topic skill acquisition, while others are more focused on the concepts that are needed to make sense of the mathematics being studied. But it may be hard to tell which approach a textbook takes from a simple read-through of its table of contents. In Exercise 1, you'll explore your own textbook's mathematical framing with respect to big ideas and think about the value of identifying big ideas in your curriculum materials.

Working through problems in your textbook can provide insights into the big math ideas tapped by the problems.

If you don't use a textbook but instead find and/or create your own materials for the majority of your lessons, then you're basically working from your own mathematical framework. In this case, you can use this exercise to explicitly articulate that framework for yourself (if you haven't done so already). Whether you use commercial curriculum materials or not, it's useful to be explicit about how that framework relates to the big mathematical concepts that underlie your curriculum.

Process for Analyzing Your Textbook. Follow the steps below to complete Exercise 1. Read through all the steps before you begin in order to get an overview of the process.

Step 1:
Choose
a unit
from your
textbook.

Step 2:
Make a copy
of Chapter 4
Worksheet 1:
"Examining
Your
Textbook."

Step 1: **Choose a unit from your textbook.** Use whatever criteria you want for making your choice. You may want to work with the unit you're currently using or the one that's coming up next. If you're using this book in a study group that includes grade-level colleagues, you may choose to select a unit jointly. If your textbook isn't organized into units, choose two or three consecutive chapters to investigate.

Step 2: **Make a copy of Chapter 4 Worksheet 1: "Examining Your Textbook."** Make a copy of the blank Chapter 4 Worksheet 1: "Examining Your Textbook," which is located in the Appendix and as a writeable PDF on PDToolKit (see Figure 4.1). Think about the kind of information you will need to be looking for to fill out the worksheet. Have some paper on hand for making notes and jotting down noteworthy examples as you work with your textbook unit.

Figure 4.1   Blank Chapter 4 Worksheet 1

Chapter 4 Worksheet 1: Examining Your Textbook

Unit Title:	
What key concepts (big ideas) does the unit focus on?	Thoughts/Comments:
What key knowledge and skills does the unit emphasize?	Thoughts/Comments:

Chapter Title:	
What key concepts (big ideas) does this chapter focus on?	Thoughts/Comments:
How does the work in this chapter engage mathematical practices/ habits of mind?	Thoughts/Comments:
What key knowledge and skills does this chapter emphasize?	Thoughts/Comments:
What are the explicit connections to other chapters in the unit?	Thoughts/Comments:

Copyright © Pearson Education

PDToolkit
for
*Examining Mathematics
Practice through
Classroom Artifacts*

Step 3: **Read the unit introduction in the teacher guide.** If the individual chapters have introductions as well, read those too. Note how the authors frame the mathematics that the unit addresses and describe the mathematical goals of the unit, using supporting evidence.

Step 4: **Review the chapters for the unit.** Using your teacher guide, scan the individual chapters to see how the math develops throughout the unit. Look at some individual lessons within each chapter as well to get a sense of the kind of mathematical thinking students are asked to do. Jot down notes to help you fill out the "Examining Your Textbook" worksheet.

Step 5: **Complete the worksheet.** Be sure to include some examples from the textbook as evidence for your observations and comments.

Step 6: **Reflect on your work.** If you're working on your own, use your worksheet to help answer the study questions that follow. If you're working with others, take some time to discuss your analysis, using your completed worksheet and the study questions to help guide your conversation. Share some of the examples you chose from your textbook to support your observations. If you and your colleagues chose different units (or are even analyzing different textbooks), you might want to explore similarities and differences in your observations. A short discussion about using mathematical frameworks to analyze textbooks follows the study questions. You may also want to refer to this discussion in your reflection/discussion.

Step 3:
Read the unit introduction in the teacher guide.

Step 4:
Review the chapters for the unit.

Step 5:
Complete the worksheet.

Step 6:
Reflect on your work.

Study Questions

▶ What kind of mathematical perspective do the authors use to frame the unit?

- What is the mathematical focus of the unit?
  - How clearly is this focus articulated for the teacher?
  - How clearly is this focus articulated for the student?
- How do the authors connect skill development to underlying concepts?
- How do the authors emphasize the use of mathematical practices?

▶ What is the "mathematical story line" of the unit/chapter—how does the mathematics develop from the unit/chapter's beginning to its closing?

- How do the authors address and develop the mathematical concepts at the core of the unit?
- What mathematical connections does the textbook make among chapters in the unit?

▶ If your textbook does not help you identify big ideas, where do you see opportunities to emphasize them yourself?

Commentary on Exercise 1. The observations we make in this discussion section are, by necessity, rather general because we can't tailor them to the specifics of individual textbooks. However, here are some brief comments about the study questions.

How Do the Authors Frame the Unit/Chapter from a Mathematical Perspective?

The more explicit your textbook is about the important mathematical ideas driving the curriculum, the easier it will be for you to make sure that you're providing students with rigorous mathematical experiences. Some textbooks are obviously focused around big ideas, while others may be built with similarly strong conceptual underpinnings but have more traditional organizations and conventions for naming units and chapters that make these underpinnings more challenging to identify. Still others are driven more by a procedural framing of the mathematics than by a conceptual one.

You can often distinguish between texts where big ideas figure in heavily and ones that are more about topics and procedures by the ways in which lessons and chapters flow. Does your textbook present a specific problem-solving approach, provide opportunities for practice, and then move on? Chances are that it's not very conceptually driven. Textbooks that have a more conceptual framework tend to provide more time for students to investigate mathematical situations and make sense of different ways to represent them. A more conceptually driven framing will also be reflected in the following:

- Attention to concepts and processes in teacher notes and lessons themselves
- Emphasis on students' justification of their thinking (a kind of "proto-proof") rather than just step-by-step descriptions of their solutions
- Emphasis on connections within and across ideas, chapters, and/or units

If you find that your textbook is relatively silent in articulating big ideas, you can think about ways to draw these out on your own. You can look to resources like the CCSS to help you examine your textbook through the lens of critical areas of mathematical knowledge.

What Is the Mathematical Story Line of the Unit/Chapter? This question relates to mathematical coherence. For some textbooks, there may actually be little discernible coherence. For others, coherence might exist at an organizational rather than a conceptual level. For example, a textbook might have a unit on multiplication that includes chapters about multiplication of whole numbers and multiplication of decimal numbers, followed by a corresponding unit on division. The two units might share similar structures without drawing explicit connections between the two operations or relationships between the kinds of problems that students solve in each unit.

Other textbooks seek to make explicit conceptual connections both through the structure and organization of the materials and through notes and instructions to the teacher. These textbooks will have a more explicit mathematical story line that helps to map out the ideas that students will be working on during the unit (and perhaps across units as well). Textbooks with a clear mathematical story line can be particularly useful for seeing where students' current understanding fits in the overall development of the mathematics and also for getting a picture of the kinds of conceptual supports students may need as the mathematical ideas unfold during the unit.

One potential pitfall of these efforts to create coherence is that the connections can be overlooked or misunderstood by someone used to thinking topically, particularly if the text uses a variety of representations to convey the same underlying idea. Recall the vignette from the beginning of the chapter. Jasmine saw the lessons in her new textbook as a jumble of disconnected activities rather than a suite of activities about adding by fives. When teachers like Jasmine fail to see the big ideas that drive a unit, their instruction typically focuses on students' mastery of the different representations in the disparate lessons (e.g., counting on a number line, learning the value of coins, or telling time) rather than on the underlying mathematical idea.

The more that your textbook helps to articulate the unit's conceptual story line, the easier it should be for you to make connections (for yourself and for your students) between specific lesson activities and the mathematical ideas underpinning—and driving—the work. If textbook materials don't explicitly make these connections, we suggest that you try to do so as part of your lesson planning. Use some of your planning time to think about the lesson from a conceptual as well as a logistical perspective and ask yourself questions like the following:

- What are the mathematical ideas I want to emphasize in the lesson?
- How will these ideas help me shape my goals for the lesson?
- How might I respond to students during the lesson to promote these ideas?

Stepping Back. The big idea of Exercise 1 is that analyzing curriculum materials in terms of a big ideas framework can help you keep your attention focused on important mathematical ideas during lessons. The more you understand how your math program builds conceptual understanding, the better shape you're in to use the program well. Whether the focus on big ideas is built into the curriculum materials themselves or comes from your own analysis and interpretation of the materials, there is an advantage to using this framework. It helps you to better diagnose and address students' learning needs and to promote deep and flexible math understanding.

Now that we've investigated the mathematical framing used by your textbook at the unit and chapter levels, let's drop down to using the big ideas and habits of mind/practices frameworks at the individual lesson level. When you get right down to it, this is where the rubber really meets the road since students build their mathematical understanding and skill and their ideas about themselves as mathematical learners through their daily work.

Exercise 2: A Tale of Two Lessons—Using Mathematical Frameworks to Think About Rigor and Cognitive Demand

One of the reasons to treat textbook lessons as artifacts for study is to investigate their potential for rigorous mathematics. We can use the big ideas and practices/habits of mind frameworks to support this inquiry. The big ideas framework offers a perspective on whether (and how) lessons promote conceptual understanding. The practices/habits of mind framework focuses on the ways in which lessons cultivate the processing and communication skills that characterize disciplinary-based thinking—what many researchers and educators describe as "doing math." Taken together, these frameworks help us consider the cognitive demands of the tasks students encounter in class.

Cognitively demanding tasks are complex and nonroutine and engage students' conceptual understanding. They make room for different ways of arriving at a solution and often require using (and drawing connections among) different representations and solution strategies. Because they have an element of novelty to them, tasks that are cognitively demanding require students to make connections to other situations, ideas, and representations that are already familiar to them. They're also designed to engage students as independent thinkers, leaving some of the work of analyzing the task, planning a line of attack, and assessing the effectiveness of the plan to the students themselves. Cognitively demanding tasks are, well, *demanding*. They're neither simple nor straightforward, and they require persistence and a willingness to regroup, identify other approaches, and give them a try if current methods don't seem to be fruitful (Henningsen & Stein, 1997; Smith & Stein, 1998; Stein, Grover, & Henningsen, 1996; Stein, Smith, Henningsen, & Silver, 2009).

In Exercise 2, we'll consider the mathematical rigor of two lesson plans about fact families.

Process for Analyzing the Lessons. Follow the steps below to complete Exercise 2. Read through all the steps before you begin in order to get an overview of the process.

Step 1: **Make two copies of Chapter 4 Worksheet 2: "Analyzing a Lesson."** You'll use the first copy for Lesson Plan #1 (*Fact Family Houses*) and the second for Lesson Plan #2 (*Fact Families*). The blank worksheet is located in the Appendix and as a writeable PDF on PDToolKit (see Figure 4.2). You may also wish to make copies of the two lesson plans themselves (Figure 4.3 and 4.4) so you can make notes on them.

Step 2: **Read Lesson Plan #1: "Fact Family Houses."** This lesson was designed for a 45-minute class (see Figure 4.3).

Step 3: **Complete Chapter 4 Worksheet 2 for Lesson Plan #1.** Make note of the aspects of the lesson that provided evidence for your responses on the worksheet. In the column labeled "Cognitive Demands of the Task," note the kind of work students are asked to do. For example:

- Is the task a routine or nonroutine one?
- How does it engage students' conceptual knowledge?

Step 4: **Read Lesson Plan #2: "Fact Families."** This is a lesson designed for a 60-minute class (see Figure 4.4).

Step 1: Make two copies of Chapter 4 Worksheet 2: "Analyzing a Lesson."

Step 2: Read Lesson Plan #1: "Fact Family Houses."

Step 3: Complete Chapter 4 Worksheet 2 for Lesson Plan #1.

Step 4: Read Lesson Plan #2: "Fact Families."

PDToolkit
for
*Examining Mathematics
Practice through
Classroom Artifacts*

F i g u r e 4 . 2   Lesson Plan #1: "Fact Family Houses"

Chapter 4 Worksheet 2: Analyzing a Lesson
Lesson:

Task	Math Skills Emphasized?	Math Concepts Emphasized?	Math Practices/ Habits of Mind Emphasized?	Task Demands
Activity 1:				
Activity 2:				
Activity 3:				
Activity 4:				

Figure 4.3 Lesson Plan #1: "Fact Families Houses"

Lesson plan

Materials:

◆ Dice (two per student)
◆ "Fact Family Houses" worksheets.

The Lesson:

1. Whole-class demonstration

◆ Write the following fact family on the board:

$$4 + 3 = 7 \qquad 7 - 4 = 3$$
$$3 + 4 = 7 \qquad 7 - 3 = 4$$

◆ Tell your students that a fact family is composed of four related number sentences. Show the class how to make a fact family house:

—Draw a house with a roof, two windows, and a garden.

—Put the addends in the window and the sum on the roof

—Put the four number sentences in the garden

◆ Make another fact family house as a class. This time, roll two dice to find the two addends.

2. Individual work

◆ Pass out materials to each child. Have students make their own fact family houses, using the numbers they roll as addends. Make sure that students write the fact family number sentences in the garden.

◆ See how many different fact family houses each child can make correctly. Children also love to be creative and decorate the houses and gardens.

3. Whole-group sharing

◆ Leave five minutes at the end of class for students to share some of their fact family houses.

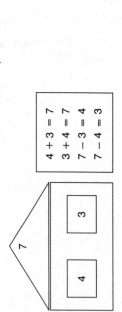

| 4 | 3 |

7

| 4 + 3 = 7 |
| 3 + 4 = 7 |
| 7 − 3 = 4 |
| 7 − 4 = 3 |

Student worksheet

Fact Family Houses

NAME_____   DATE_____

Roll your dice and record the numbers in the windows. Put the sum on the roof. Write the four fact family number sentences in the garden.

Complete as many houses as you can!

Figure 4.4   Lesson Plan #2: "Fact Families"

Lesson plan

Materials for class:

Demonstration dominoes, dominoes (three for each pair of students), "Fact Families" worksheets.

Prepare two or three demonstration dominoes that have both a "regular" domino and one that isn't divided.

Lesson activities:

1. Demonstration (whole class)

—Fold a demonstration domino so only the regular domino shows. Ask students to describe the number of dots they see. Unfold the domino to illustrate that the two groups of dots also make a larger whole. (The domino above has three dots on the left, two on the right, and five all together.)

—Repeat with one or two more dominoes as needed to make sure that students "see" the two parts and the whole.

2. Finding parts and wholes (pair work)

—Pass out three dominoes to each pair and worksheets to every student.

—For each domino, students are to record the dots and write number sentences describing the domino. Ask students to see how many number sentences they can find.

—Students then use their work to develop conjectures about what's always true about number sentences for dominoes. They record their conjectures on their worksheets.

3. Class discussion (whole group)

—Ask several pairs of students to write their number sentences on the board. As a class, discuss observations and conjectures about the number sentences. Bring out the following ideas in your discussion:

- If you know any two numbers in the number sentence, you can find the third
- Connections among the four members of the fact family
- Addition and subtraction undo each other

4. Further practice (whole group)

—Pick a domino. Tell the class you'll say two of the numbers on the domino and they should tell you what the third number could be. Note that you might tell them the two parts or you might say the whole and one of the parts.

—Continue with different dominoes as time permits. Select numbers that will give the class practice with math facts they find challenging.

Student worksheet

Fact Families

NAME_____   DATE_____

Domino 1

Number sentences:

Domino 2

Number sentences:

Domino 3

Number sentences:

What do you think is always true about the number sentences you can make from dominoes?

1.

2.

3.

4.

← fold line

79

Step 5: **Complete Chapter 4 Worksheet 2 for Lesson Plan #2.** As you did with the "Fact Family Houses" lesson plan, jot down notes about the aspects of the "Fact Families" lesson plan that provide evidence for your observations and comments.

Step 6: **Reflect on your work.** If you're working with others, take a few minutes to share and discuss your analysis of the two lessons. Use the study questions and completed sample worksheets (Tables 4.2 and 4.3) to help you reflect on your observations and start your discussion. As always, use the sample worksheets as stimulus for your own reflections and discussion, not as *the* way to complete them.Study Questions

Step 5:
Complete Chapter 4 Worksheet 2 for Lesson Plan #2.

Step 6:
Reflect on your work.

Study Questions

► Compare and contrast the two lessons in terms of their mathematical rigor. Use examples to support your analysis of how the lessons engage big ideas and mathematical habits of mind and practices.

► How might you change either of these lessons to increase the level of rigor?

  ▪ What about your suggested changes increases the rigor of the task?

  ▪ How do your suggested changes relate to the two mathematical frameworks we've been discussing?

► How do the student worksheets for the two lessons compare in terms of the kind of information they might reveal about students' thinking?

Commentary on Exercise 2. While both of these lessons focus on addition and subtraction fact families, they ask students to do very different work. The "Fact Family Houses" lesson focuses on computational practice, using a task that is routine and relatively simple. The "Fact Families" lesson, in contrast, is more mathematically demanding. It's designed to engage students in observing, reasoning, and conjecturing, and it explicitly attends to conceptual development, emphasizing the inverse relationship between addition and subtraction.

While the "Fact Family Houses" lesson tells students how to identify related number sentences, "Fact Families" leaves it to students to decide what their number sentences will look like and how many number sentences there are to find. By asking students to define important elements of their work, develop conjectures from their observations, and discuss these conjectures with others, the "Fact Families" task asks students to engage in mathematical practices associated with "doing math."

The differences between students' opportunities for mathematical thinking in the two lesson activities are also reflected in the accompanying worksheets.

CCSS–Grade 2
Represent and solve problems involving addition and subtraction. p. 18.

CCSS–Mathematical Practices
Make sense of problems and persevere in solving them. p. 6.
Reason abstractly and quantitatively. p. 6.
Model with mathematics. p. 7.
Look for and make use of structure. p. 8.

TABLE 4.2 Completed Sample Worksheet: "Fact Family Houses" Lesson Plan

Task	Math Skills Emphasized?	Math Concepts Emphasized?	Math Practices/ Habits of Mind Emphasized?	Cognitive Demands of the Task
Activity 1: Teacher introduction	Math facts: addition and subtraction	Fact families are a set of related number sentences	None	Routine procedure Teacher does most of the work
Activity 2: Individual work: make fact family houses	Math facts	Fact families are a set of related number sentences	None	Follow a well-specified procedure Practice math facts Single (numerical) representation
Activity 3: Share work	Math facts	None	Communication	Students share their work

TABLE 4.3 Completed Sample Worksheet: "Fact Families" Lesson Plan

Task	Math Skills Emphasized?	Math Concepts Emphasized?	Math Practices/Habits of Mind Emphasized?	Cognitive Demands of the Task
Activity 1: Teacher introduction	Math facts (addition and subtraction)	Relationship among parts and whole in addition and subtraction	None	Students make observations about the dominoes
Activity 2: Work in pairs on worksheet	Math facts	Relationship among parts and whole	Observe relationships among the parts of the domino that will lead to finding number sentences Look for all relevant number sentences for each domino Look for patterns Make conjectures Communicate thinking	Nonroutine Requires students to do some analysis of task and make decisions about producing number sentences Engages math processes and habits of mind Uses two representations (dominoes and number sentences) Asks students to communicate their thinking
Activity 3: Whole-group discussion	Math facts	Relationship between addition and subtraction Inverses undo each other If you know two parts of the "family," you can compute the third	Make observations Make comparisons Find connections Make conjectures Communicate thinking	Engages conceptual understanding Engages math processes and habits of mind Asks students to communicate their thinking
Activity 4: Find possible third number on the domino	Math facts	Relationship among parts and whole	Interpret Use patterns and conceptual understanding to make conjectures	Multiple possible solutions Engages conceptual understanding Engages math processes and habits of mind

The "Fact Family Houses" worksheet guides students to find four number sentences for each fact family. It further guides students to find two addition sentences and two subtraction sentences by providing the operation signs for students. While some students may benefit from having such a clear organizational structure, the worksheet constrains the ways students are likely to think about the connections between the numbers they roll on the dice and the number sentences they write. (One possible exception to this would be if students rolled a pair of identical numbers—would four number sentences still hold in this case?) The "Fact Families" worksheet is more open-ended, leaving it up to the students to figure out which number sentences reflect the domino parts and whole and how many sentences there are to be for each domino. It also encourages students to use their observations to look for regularities that might be generalizable.

General Commentary on Using Mathematical Frameworks to Consider Mathematical Rigor

It shouldn't come as any surprise that the more rigorous students' mathematics education, the greater their achievement (Resnick & Zurawsky, 2006). A steady diet of lessons that simply ask students to memorize and reproduce facts, procedures, and strategies on cue will not support the development of flexible or resourceful thinkers—and such a bland diet is likely to be less interesting and engaging to students as well. The big ideas and mathematical practices/habits of mind frameworks provide ways to analyze the "nutritional content" and key ingredients of the lessons you teach, offering approaches for identifying the important mathematical goals of lessons and anticipating the kinds of thinking we hope to promote in class.

The kind of task you use in class affects the richness of the thinking you get to see among your students. If you were to teach the "Fact Family Houses" lesson as it's written, for example, the only evidence of students' thinking you might be able to access is on their completed worksheets. The worksheets are unlikely to provide you much information about whether your students recognize or understand the relationships among the sentences in a fact family, whether they see that addition and subtraction undo each other, or whether they simply filled in the worksheet mechanically and without much thought at all. Furthermore, the vague (and possibly 11th-hour) instructions in the lesson plan for a whole-group discussion mean that students would not necessarily get the chance to consider their own ideas in light of their classmates' thinking.

But it's also the case that teachers can lower (or raise) the mathematical rigor of a lesson plan by the way they teach it in class. Henningsen and Stein (1997) reported that, over the course of a lesson, teachers they studied lowered the cognitive demand of more than 60 percent of tasks that were initially rated as highly demanding. They noted that some of the very characteristics of demanding (and therefore rigorous) tasks—their relative complexity, open-endedness, and emphasis on students' making and using mathematical observations—make them more challenging to teach. Students (and teachers, too) can find these kinds of lessons ambiguous, confusing, and just plain hard enough that it can often be easier and more comfortable to make them simpler and more straightforward (and therefore less cognitively demanding). But because the high cognitive demand makes these the very kinds of tasks that build the deep and flexible mathematical thinking mathematics educators endorse, it's worth it to really try to stay the course and provide structures and supports for students to engage in work that will build their conceptual knowledge and develop their mathematical practices and habits of mind.

If you can't identify many lessons in your textbook that engage students in cognitively demanding work, you probably want to think about how you can either alter them or find additional tasks that *will* provide students the opportunity for more conceptual thinking and mathematical investigation. For example, if your textbook is heavier on routine practice than on concept development, consider adding more conceptual focus to those routine tasks students work on. One approach would be to make them more open ended so that students have more of a chance to explore the mathematics and also to make more of the decisions about how they will approach the task. The big ideas and habits of mind guiding frameworks we discussed earlier can help with this process.

Using Mathematical Frameworks in Your Lessons

We end this chapter by encouraging you to think about ways to integrate the use of mathematical frameworks in your own work. Here are some ideas that you might want to try.

Lesson Planning. When you plan lessons, identify the big ideas that drive the activities outlined in your textbook. How do lesson activities call on and support conceptual understanding? Ask yourself, too, about the opportunities that activities offer students for engaging in mathematical processes, practices, and ways the of thinking. Answering these questions can help you decide whether you want to beef up the mathematics of a lesson and/or focus it more sharply on particular mathematical ideas and processes.

- Analyze the conceptual demands of the lesson activities. Do they offer opportunities for students to engage in conceptual thinking? If so, what are the big ideas at play? If not, how might you adapt activities to help students develop the conceptual thinking that lies at the heart of a rigorous mathematical education? How do you plan to keep these big ideas at the forefront of your instruction?

- Think about how the lesson will encourage students to develop mathematical practices and habits of mind. Look for opportunities for students to make observations, use different tools and representations, look for general patterns and/or rules, propose and test conjectures, justify their thinking, and more.

- Plan for opportunities to check on students' understanding of the relevant big ideas. By thinking about when and how you will check in with students about their understanding, you'll be able to closely monitor their learning and make well-informed instructional decisions.

- As you did in Chapter 3, anticipate possible conceptual errors and/or challenges and think about how you might respond to them.

Teaching the Lesson. Keep your eye on the big ideas that you have determined are central to the lesson and look for opportunities to help students articulate and connect important mathematical concepts. When anticipated misunderstandings or partial understandings emerge, think about how to use them as opportunities to address the big ideas. As students work, look for ways to promote their developing and exercising mathematical practices and habits of mind. In addition, encourage them to explain, justify, and share their thinking so that you can make sure that you have a good diagnostic handle on how they're thinking about important mathematical ideas.

Wrapping Up

This chapter offered you a chance to examine how big ideas play out within a lesson and across a unit of study and also to investigate how curriculum materials can engage mathematical practices and habits of mind. The big ideas and mathematical practices/habits of mind frameworks provide lenses through which you can view the mathematical content of your curriculum materials and of classroom artifacts you may choose to analyze as well. The more you become skilled at using these lenses to examine mathematical tasks (and students' work on tasks), the more you will be prepared to keep an eye on rigorous mathematics.

Choosing, Using, and Connecting
Mathematical Representations

After reading chapter 9 in the book *Elementary and Middle School Mathematics: Teaching Developmentally* by John van de Walle (2004), Ms. Ridgeway became motivated to help her first-grade students develop a more flexible understanding of numbers and their relationships. She's decided to focus on three types of experiences and representations involving numbers 1 to 10 that van de Walle emphasizes.

Spatial relationships: Ms. Ridgeway wants to help her students recognize the sizes of sets of objects in patterned arrangements without counting them. She plans on using visual patterns to distinguish common groupings while building on students' experiences with dice games (see Figure 5.1).

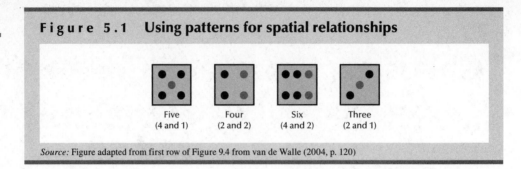

F i g u r e 5 . 1   Using patterns for spatial relationships

Five
(4 and 1)

Four
(2 and 2)

Six
(4 and 2)

Three
(2 and 1)

Source: Figure adapted from first row of Figure 9.4 from van de Walle (2004, p. 120)

Counting on (and back) one or two counts: She also wants to help her students examine how one number is related to another. For example, 5 is one more than 4, and it's also two less than 7. She thinks that using representations such as arrows, words, and color can help point students to the relationships of one and two more and one and two less (see Figure 5.2).

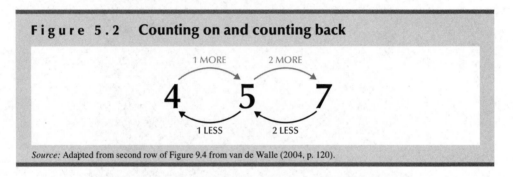

F i g u r e 5 . 2   Counting on and counting back

1 MORE   2 MORE

4   5   7

1 LESS   2 LESS

Source: Adapted from second row of Figure 9.4 from van de Walle (2004, p. 120).

Benchmark numbers of 5 and 10: Ms. Ridgeway thinks it's important to help her students relate a given number to benchmarks of 5 or 10. She's planning on using 5-frame and 10-frame representations to help them focus on visualizing these relationships to these benchmark quantities (see Figure 5.3).

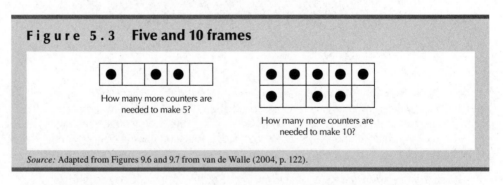

F i g u r e 5 . 3   Five and 10 frames

How many more counters are
needed to make 5?

How many more counters are
needed to make 10?

Source: Adapted from Figures 9.6 and 9.7 from van de Walle (2004, p. 122).

Ms. Ridgeway wants to plan a variety of activities that utilize these three types of relationships and their corresponding representations in order to develop her students' flexibility with number and operations. Because she's already had her students play games involving dice, she knows that students are familiar with the arrangements of dots on the faces of a die. She therefore decides to use dice to begin working on spatial arrangements, focusing initially on the numbers 1 to 6. She uses gray and black dots to help students visualize the distinction between the sets of numbers (4 and 1, 2 and 2, 4 and 2, and so on) She plans to use both a strategy and different representations to help her students count on and count back (examine one and two more and one and two less by counting forward and backward and representing this with arrows, numbers, and words). Finally, she wants her students to utilize benchmark numbers of 5 and 10 in thinking about the various combinations of numbers. She has similar plans to use different representations to help students understand connections between counting up/down and the relationships between numbers and useful benchmarks.

In this vignette, Ms. Ridgeway used her knowledge of her students, of the math content, and of different ways to represent the content to create an overall plan for the types of experiences she wanted to provide her first-grade students. Like Ms. Ridgeway, as teachers we work constantly to try and bring students to a better understanding of the content we teach. Ms. Ridgeway used representations as tools for providing her students visual access to the number relationships she wanted her students to understand.

Representations can be extremely powerful tools because they can be both process and product—a student's act (or process) of representing a mathematical concept in some form (e.g., using dots and color to show how a number can be decomposed) and the resulting product itself (e.g., notations, diagrams, graphical displays, and symbolic expressions). Part of the power of mathematics is the way that ideas can be expressed in many forms: symbols, graphs, charts, counters, dots, number lines, area models, fraction strips, 10 frames, hundreds charts, and so on.

Unfortunately, quite often "product" representations are taught as procedures and learned as ends in themselves rather than as tools for capturing important mathematical aspects of problems and their solutions. For example, students can be asked to create a table without asking them to think about how to analyze the relationship across the columns within a row. When we ask students to focus on the procedures for creating representations rather than on understanding the mathematical relationships captured within them, we're doing them a disservice because we are separating representations from their mathematical meaning. Instead, it's important for children to develop the flexibility to move from one representation to another and to choose and use representations as problem-solving tools that aid in understanding mathematical concepts.

The power and importance of representations was highlighted in the *Principles and Standards* of the National Council of Teachers of Mathematics (NCTM):

> Students should understand that written representations of mathematical ideas are an essential part of learning and doing mathematics. It is important to encourage students to represent their ideas in ways that make sense to them, even if their first representations are not conventional ones. It is also important that they learn conventional forms of representation to facilitate both their learning of mathematics and their communication with others about mathematical ideas. The fact that representations are such effective tools may obscure how difficult it was to develop them and, more important, how much work it takes to understand them. (NCTM, 2000, p. 67)

The Common Core State Standards (CCSS) highlight the interweaving of representations and conceptual understanding of content. Beginning in kindergarten and continuing through grade 4, the CCSS focus on representing, relating, and operating on whole numbers while highlighting the importance of representing and solving problems. In grade 6, the focus moves to representing and analyzing quantitative relationships among rational numbers (CCSS, 2010).

There is an increasing awareness in the mathematics education community that representation is closely linked with students' understanding. Teachers need opportunities to understand how students use representations to guide their problem solving and to learn how to help their students analyze one another's solutions (and representations) as a means of deepening their mathematical understanding. When provided with these opportunities, teachers can develop more differentiated, representation-rich, and flexible approaches to the mathematics for themselves and their students (Seago & Goldsmith, 2006).

Classroom artifacts can provide various types of representations for us to examine. These representations can give us windows into students' thinking and reasoning. Different types of artifacts can afford access to different kinds of representations. For example, written student work can let us examine static representations, such as the types of algorithms that students use, records of their calculations, their written explanations, or pictures, tables, graphs, or diagrams that students use to represent and solve problems. Video can capture all of these and more. Because it can record students' work as it unfolds, we can use video to examine students' verbal explanations, their use of manipulatives while working on math tasks, and also the ways they use physical gestures to model a mathematical point—for example, representing an angle measure or growth pattern (Sherin, 2004).

General Commentary About Representations

The mathematical demands of teaching are many and often underappreciated. The work teachers do in selecting and using representations with students is part of a *specialized mathematical knowledge* that is unique to teaching (Ball & Bass, 2000; Ball, Thames, & Phelps, 2008; Shulman, 1986). Deborah Ball and her colleagues contend that teachers must hold a special type of mathematical knowledge—a knowledge that is not demanded by others who use mathematics in their professional lives (e.g., research mathematicians or engineers). The mathematical work teachers do every day involves more than just understanding the content for themselves; it involves figuring out how to make content accessible and visible to their students, like Ms. Ridgeway did. Ms. Ridgeway's decisions about the math ideas that were important for her students to understand and the particular kinds of experiences that would be likely to promote that understanding required her to draw on a very specific and detailed type of mathematical knowledge. In particular, she needed to recognize how each of the representations she selected would help to highlight key mathematical relationships.

89

Chapter 5

**Choosing,
Using, and
Connecting
Mathematical
Representations**

The kinds of manipulatives (and other representations)
students use to solve problems can highlight different
aspects of the underlying mathematics.

In regard to representations, mathematics teaching often requires you to do the
following:

- **Select representations for particular purposes**—Figure out which representations are
  most likely to support your students' access to and conceptualization of the content.

- **Recognize the mathematics involved in using a particular representation**—Ascertain
  what a representation offers mathematically and how to use it most effectively with your
  students. You also need to think about the mathematical ideas a particular representation
  might fail to highlight (or even obscure) and to think about whether additional representations are necessary to help students access the mathematics more fully.

- **Link representations to underlying ideas and to other representations**—Connect
  various representations to the mathematical ideas they represent and to compare and
  contrast various representations.

This chapter is designed to support you in using classroom artifacts to interpret and
describe the representations that students choose and use.

Exercises

As you work through the exercises in this chapter, you'll have the opportunity to practice describing, analyzing, and finding connections among different representations. The
exercises are intended to support you in the examination of various representations as they
emerge in classroom artifacts. The chapter includes three exercises. Each exercise uses a
different classroom artifact, and each offers the chance to practice examining, observing,
and interpreting a variety of representations. The first exercise presents a classroom scenario
of a seventh-grade lesson about identifying and generalizing a pattern. Exercises 2 and 3 are

included at the end of the chapter. Exercise 2 is based on a video clip from an upper elementary fraction lesson, and Exercise 3 uses a set of student representations from a third-grade geometry/measurement problem focusing on the concept of area and perimeter.

We've provided information about the grade levels of the three lessons in the chapter to give you some sense of context for the associated representations, but the tasks themselves are appropriate for a wide grade range. Students from elementary to high school can productively work on the problems in the exercises; the differences often lay in the ways that students of different ages and levels of development think about—and represent—the problem space. In these exercises, we'd like you to focus on the types of representations that emerge in these particular artifacts rather than on the grade levels. Representations emerge in all grade levels across all content areas and are a critical component of teaching and learning mathematics.

Exercise 1: Larry's Seventh-Grade Classroom Scenario

The following scenario offers a means of examining how classroom artifacts can capture a variety of representations. It also illustrates how Larry, a seventh-grade teacher, faces the challenge of interpreting students' mathematical ideas and representations as they emerge during a lesson.

Larry was excited to have his students work on the new problem that he got at a workshop on making algebra more accessible to students. With his state's increasing demand to teach algebra to all students, he worries that the standard methods and problems he has been using for years are not helping the majority of his students gain an understanding of basic algebra concepts. He's going to have them work on a problem that was adapted from a sixth-grade Japanese lesson that Larry found intriguing. He really likes this problem as a way to help students conceptualize ideas about slope and the y-intercept that go beyond graphing lines and finding "rise over run." After solving the problem himself and thinking about how his students would approach it, Larry posed the "Growing Dots" problem to his students (see Figure 5.4).

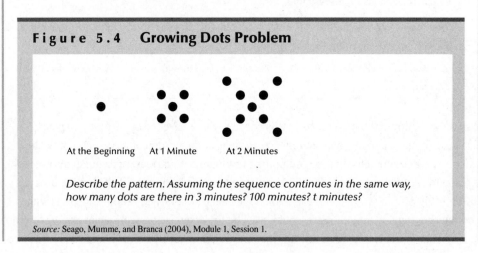

Figure 5.4   Growing Dots Problem

At the Beginning   At 1 Minute   At 2 Minutes

Describe the pattern. Assuming the sequence continues in the same way, how many dots are there in 3 minutes? 100 minutes? t minutes?

Source: Seago, Mumme, and Branca (2004), Module 1, Session 1.

91

Chapter 5

**Choosing,
Using, and
Connecting
Mathematical
Representations**

As Larry walked around to observe his students working, he was surprised at the variety of ways in which students were approaching the problem. He had anticipated that they would each make a table and never imagined the visual approaches that he observed them using. On further analysis, he realized that the variety of students' solutions really boiled down to four main types, or methods (see Figure 5.5).

Figure 5.5   Solutions from Larry's class

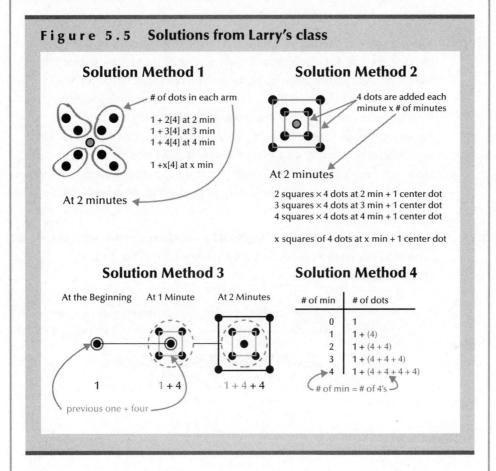

As Larry began to interpret these approaches more carefully, he realized that there was much more mathematics embedded within this problem and these methods than he originally thought. While these were four distinct methods and ways of thinking about the problem, they were also four different ways to represent how the parts of the pattern were growing. He was happy that it was the end of the class so that he could examine these methods and representations more carefully and think about how to use the different representations to drive the discussion tomorrow.

Step 1:
Identify the
key math
ideas and
examine the
four solution
methods.

Step 2:
Make a copy
of the blank
Chapter 5
worksheet
and fill in
the "Math-
ematical
Task"
column.

Step 3:
Fill in the
"Representa-
tions/
Approaches"
column
of the
worksheet.

Process for Analyzing Larry's Classroom Scenario. Follow the steps below as you complete the exercise. Read through all the steps before you begin in order to get an overview of the process.

Step 1: **Identify the key mathematical ideas and examine the four solution methods.** Take a few minutes to think about the key ideas involved in this task. Then examine carefully the four different methods/representations. You may want to work this problem out yourself and also try each method to get a better sense of the reasoning behind each.

Step 2: **Make a copy of the blank Chapter 5 worksheet and fill in the "Mathematical Task" column.** Make a copy of the blank Chapter 5 worksheet (see Figure 5.6; a blank worksheet is located in the Appendix and as a writeable PDF on PDToolKit). Fill in this column by recording the Dots problem and noting the key mathematical ideas likely to be at play for seventh-grade students. (Since, as we noted above, this problem is also appropriate for younger students, you could instead identify key ideas that elementary students would encounter. However, the commentary that follows is geared toward connecting the diagrams with symbolic representations of the solution.)

Step 3: **Fill in the "Representations/Approaches" column of the worksheet.** Be sure to pay attention to the way grayscale is used in the different representations.

F i g u r e 5 . 6 Blank Chapter 5 worksheet

Chapter 5 Worksheet: Connecting Representations		
Mathematical Task (note the task and key mathematical ideas)	Representations/Approaches	Analysis and Connection of Representations

Copyright © Pearson Education

TABLE 5.1 Completed Sample Worksheet: Larry's Classroom Scenario

Mathematical Task (note the task and key mathematical ideas)	Representations/Approaches	Analysis and Connection of Representation

Mathematical Task (note the task and key mathematical ideas)

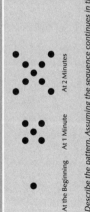

At the Beginning   At 1 Minute   At 2 Minutes

Describe the pattern. Assuming the sequence continues in the same way, how many dots are there in 3 minutes? 100 minutes? t minutes?

Key Ideas:

- Linear growth patterns describe:
  - What's changing (and how it's changing)
  - What's staying the same
  - The starting point and the constant rate of change
- Different representations can capture/describe the elements of linear growth differently
- Connections to algebra: the starting point represents the y-intercept and the constant rate of change represents the slope of a linear function

Representations/Approaches

Solution Method 1

\# of dots in each arm

1 + 2[4] at 2 min
1 + 3[4] at 3 min
1 + 4[4] at 4 min

1 + x[4] at x min

At 2 minutes

Solution Method 2

4 dots are added each
minute × # of minutes

At 2 minutes

2 squares × 4 dots at 2 min + 1 center dot
3 squares × 4 dots at 3 min + 1 center dot
4 squares × 4 dots at 4 min + 1 center dot

x squares of 4 dots at x min + 1 center dot

Analysis and Connection of Representation

This visual method represents the sequence with drawings and breaks each picture into two components: the center and the "arms." The representation emphasizes what stays the same at each minute (the center dot) and what changes (the number of dots in each arm). The number of dots in each arm corresponds to the number of minutes the pattern has been growing (i.e., two dots in each arm at two minutes, three dots in each arm at three minutes).

This visual method is similar to method 1 in that it also uses the picture and breaks it into two parts. Both methods separate the center dot from the other dots. However, the "squares" method (and representation) groups the dots into squares, with one dot at each of the vertices. The number of squares corresponds to the number of minutes the pattern has been growing (i.e., two squares at two minutes; three squares at three minutes).

Continued

93

TABLE 5.1 Completed Sample Worksheet: Larry's Classroom Scenario (continued)

Mathematical Task (note the task and key mathematical ideas)	Representations/Approaches	Analysis and Connection of Representation
	Solution Method 3 At the Beginning At 1 Minute At 2 Minutes 1 1 + 4 1 + 4 + 4 previous one + four **Solution Method 4** 	# of min	# of dots	 |---|---| 	0	1	 	1	1 + (4)	 	2	1 + (4 + 4)	 	3	1 + (4 + 4 + 4)	 	4	1 + (4 + 4 + 4 + 4)	 # of min = # of 4's	This is a recursive method—it focuses on describing the change from minute to minute (four new dots) and adds the amount changed to the number of dots in the previous minute. It does not explicitly attend to the part of pattern that remains unchanged (although the unchanging portion is accounted for in the number of dots from the previous minute). This method is strictly numeric, recording the number of dots at each minute in a table. The values in the "# of dots" column does not indicate a simple total but instead records the specific numbers and operations used to obtain the total. This representation also distinguishes between what changes and what stays the same by using two different colors (black and gray). At 0 minutes, the entry is 1 (in black). Subsequent entries maintain the separateness of the unchanging 1 and also record the number of fours that have been added at each minute (in gray). Looking across the rows, it's possible to see that the number of fours added corresponds to the number of minutes. Separating the numbers into these two parts is similar to the "squares" method (method 2). It also is related to the "recursive" method (method 3) in that 4 is added to the number of dots from the previous minute (though in this case, the use of gray indicates what is being added each time, and the starting point is indicated in black).

Step 4: **Fill in the "Analysis/Connections" column of the worksheet.** Try to be as specific as possible.

Step 5: **Reflect on your work.** If you're working with others, take a few minutes to share and discuss your analysis of the lessons. Use the study questions and completed sample worksheet (Table 5.1) to help you reflect on your observations and start your discussion. Remember that the sample worksheet is intended to stimulate your own reflections and discussion, not to be *the* way to complete the worksheet.

Step 4: Fill in the "Analysis/ Connections" column of the worksheet.

Step 5: Reflect on your work.

Study Questions

▶ How would you describe each of these four methods?

▶ How are these methods similar? How are they different?

▶ Do you see methods that seem to be related to each other? What about them makes them similar?

▶ How are these representations connected to the problem?

▶ What are the ways that the representations highlight key ideas or aspects of the problem solution?

Commentary on Larry's Class Scenario. The exploration of linear growth is about examining two elements—a starting point that stays the same (y-intercept) and a constant rate of change (slope). These four methods each get to the same answer for the problem, but they capture the growth pattern in somewhat different ways, both diagrammatically and symbolically.

Solution method 1: Arms method. The students using this visual method are focused on the picture of the dots and how it visually breaks into two distinct parts—the center and the four "arms" (see Figure 5.7). This solution highlights what stays the same at each minute (the center dot) and what changes (one more dot per arm every minute or a total of four new dots each minute).

CCSS—Grade 5

Analyze patterns and relationships. p. 34.

CCSS—Grade 6

Represent and analyze quantitative relationships between dependent and independent variables. p. 41.

Figure 5.7 Arms method

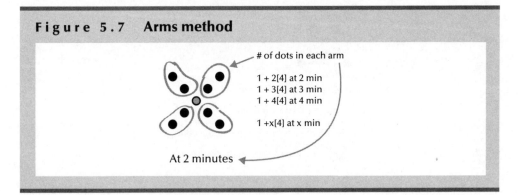

# of dots in each arm

1 + 2[4] at 2 min
1 + 3[4] at 3 min
1 + 4[4] at 4 min

1 +x[4] at x min

At 2 minutes

The visual representation of this method illuminates the students' thinking: the number of dots in each arm matches the number of minutes the pattern has been growing—at two minutes, there are two dots in each arm; at three minutes, there are three dots; and at four minutes, there are four dots. This allows students to generalize the relationship between the number of minutes and the number of dots in each arm, recognizing that there are four arms in the figure. When asked how they would represent the number of dots at 100 minutes, students using this method said, "The center dot is in the middle, and each of the four arms would be 100 dots long." A way to represent this method algebraically (symbolically) would be $1 + x(4) = $ dots (for any number of minutes x, you have one center dot + the number of dots per arm times the four arms).

Solution method 2: Squares method. Students using this visual method are thinking in a similar way to those who use the arms method in that they are using a picture and breaking it into two distinct parts (see Figure 5.8).

Both the arms and the squares methods separate the center dot from the other dots, thereby attending to both what is staying the same and what is changing as the pattern grows. However, students using the squares method (and representation) are looking at the dots as groups of squares growing out from the center dot, with one dot at each of the four corners (vertices) of the square. Since each minute "grows" another square, four dots are added each time.

The visual representation of this method and its corresponding way of thinking about the pattern focuses on the relationship between the minutes of growth and the number of squares—two squares at two minutes, three squares at three minutes, and four squares at four minutes. The student who recognizes this pattern can generalize the relationship between the number of minutes and the number of squares, recognizing that each square has four dots. When asked how they would represent the number of dots

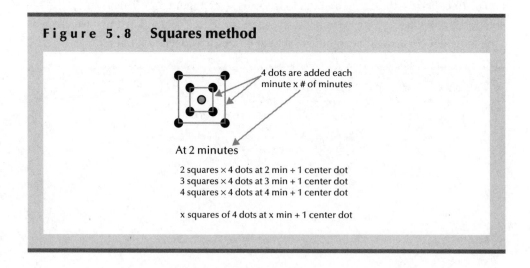

Figure 5.8   Squares method

4 dots are added each
minute x # of minutes

At 2 minutes

2 squares × 4 dots at 2 min + 1 center dot
3 squares × 4 dots at 3 min + 1 center dot
4 squares × 4 dots at 4 min + 1 center dot

x squares of 4 dots at x min + 1 center dot

at 100 minutes, students using this method said, "There's one center dot with 100 squares growing out from the center. Each square has four dots, so the pattern grows out by fours each minute." An algebraic representation of this method could be $1 + 4x =$ dots (for any number of minutes x, find the total number of dots by taking the one center dot and adding to it the number of dots in all the squares growing out from the center; each square has four dots, and the number of squares is the same as the number of minutes).

The algebraic expressions for the arms and squares methods (and for the two other methods that follow) have the same *mathematical* meaning, but they reflect different ways of thinking about—and representing—a method for solving the problem.

Arms solution: $1 + (x \times 4) =$ dots

Squares solution: $1 + (4 \times x) =$ dots

We all learned in algebra class that $4x = x4$ (for the same reason that $3 \times 4 = 4 \times 3$) and that the conventional way of representing multiplication with a variable is to put the number first and then the variable. Given this convention, the equation for both the arms and the squares methods is $1 + 4x =$ dots. But the two methods *represent* the problem solutions in rather different ways that can be captured (perhaps subtly) by the differences between thinking about "$x \times 4$" and "$4 \times x$."

CCSS—Grade 7

Use properties of operations to generate equivalent expressions. p. 47.

We recognize that most elementary teachers do not use algebraic notation with their students, so the particulars of this example may seem irrelevant to some, but the idea that students think about and represent mathematical tasks in different ways is of central importance to teachers at all levels—a big part of our jobs as teachers is to understand these different representations and to surface the important underlying mathematics by helping students make connections among them.

Solution method 3: Recursive method. The students using this method looked at the sequence of dots and focused on what changed from one minute to the next. They noticed that the pattern kept adding four dots to the previous figure at every minute (see Figure 5.9).

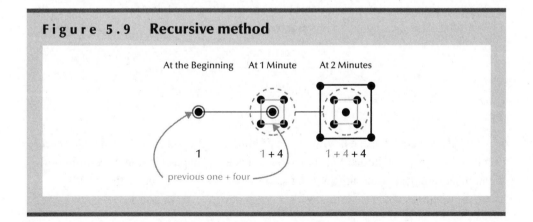

Figure 5.9   Recursive method

This method is considered a recursive way of thinking because the students are focusing on the relationship between the previous figure and the next one—how to represent the change from minute to minute. These students focus on the *growth* of the pattern—add four dots each minute—but always in reference to the previous figure. They use the number of dots from the previous minute to compute the number of dots at the next minute by adding 4 to the previous total.

Some students using this method acknowledge that the problem begins with one dot, adds four new dots at the first minute, and then continues to add four dots; others totally ignore the beginning dot and focus solely on the growth of four dots each minute. Students using a recursive method express the number of dots at 100 minutes as "add 4 more dots to the number of dots at the 99th minute." (This method, therefore, assumes that one knows or could find the number of dots from the 99th minute.)

This method involves thinking that's similar to the squares method in that both methods focus on the addition of four dots at each minute. But the two ways of thinking focus on different relationships within the picture. The recursive method focuses on looking at the change from minute to minute (you add 4), and the squares method focuses on how the number of minutes determines the number of fours you are dealing with.

Students may try to represent this recursive approach symbolically as

$$x + 4 = \text{dots}$$

where they define x to be the number of dots in the previous figure. This representation is incorrect from the perspective of algebraic notation (it requires x to be variable itself rather than to represent a variable), but it does capture some of the reasoning students use when thinking recursively. It also highlights that the students are thinking about the part of the pattern that's changing and incorporate the constant into the value of the previous figure.

However, students could generalize the pattern for any number of minutes using this approach in a nonrecursive way by thinking about how many fours they need to add for a given time. This idea could be represented as

$$1 + \underbrace{(4 + 4 + 4 + \ldots + 4 + 4)}_{x \text{ times}}$$

or

$$1 + x(4) = \text{dots}$$

That is, you start at time 0 with the beginning dot and add four more dots for each minute of change. The number of fours you add is the same as the number of minutes: the number of dots at 4 minutes is $1 + (4 \text{ minutes} \times 4)$, at 53 minutes the total is $1 + (53 \text{ minutes} \times 4)$, at 97 minutes it's $1 + (97 \text{ minutes} \times 4)$, and so on.

Solution method 4: Table method. Unlike the three previous solution types, the students using this method worked with numerical patterns rather than looking to the dots picture as the primary means for representing and solving the problem. Instead, students recorded the number of dots in a "T table" organized in two columns (# of minutes and # of dots) and then looked at the numerical relationships among the entries (see Figure 5.10).

F i g u r e 5 . 1 0   Table method

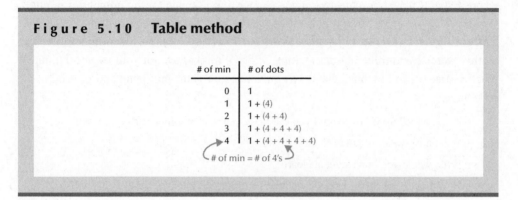

Some students simply recorded the total number of dots in the right-hand column. However, some students represented the total in an expanded notation that preserved a record of the operations involved in growing the outer layers of dots. This notation separates the center dot (the 1) from the rest of the pattern and then captures the growth by maintaining the successive addition of groups of four dots rather than compressing them into a single total. This expanded notation allows a student to see the relationship between the number of fours added and the number of minutes (i.e., to find a relationship across the columns in a row instead of just down each column). For example, the number of dots at three minutes is $1 + 4 + 4 + 4$, or the unchanging center dot plus three groups of four dots—one group for each of the three minutes.

In this representation, the use of color also plays a role by distinguishing the part of the pattern that's growing (numbers in gray) from the part that's constant (numbers in black). For example, in the "# of dots" column, the students indicated the number of dots as 1 (in black) + 4s (where the number of fours in gray correspond to the number of minutes elapsed). The students used this representation to show the pattern starting with 1 (at 0 minutes) and continuing on with what gets added each time—four more each minute. As the students added four each time, they kept the previous representation and grouped the set of fours. This allowed them to see that the number of fours at each minute was the same as the number of minutes.

Separating the numbers into these two parts reflects thinking that's similar to the thinking of students using the squares method. It's also related to the recursive method in that 4 is added to the previous figure. For an entry of 100 minutes in

the "# of minutes" column, for example, students using this expanded method
would fill in the corresponding "# of dots" column with a solution that looks like:
$1 + (4 + 4 + 4 + 4 + \ldots + 4)$—with 100 fours in the parentheses (or some other way
of notating this amount, such as "$1 + (100 \text{ fours})$"). Students might then represent this
algebraically as

$$1 + 4x = \text{dots}$$

where 4 stands for the minute-by-minute change and x stands for the number of minutes.

Reflecting on Exercise 1: Implications for Practice. Take a few minutes to reflect
on this exercise and think about the implications it might have for your own teaching
practice. Use the following questions as guidelines for your individual and/or group
reflections:

- If you were Larry, how would you use these methods in tomorrow's discussion?
- What purpose would they serve?
- What would you hope students learn?
- How do you use different representations in your classroom?

We've also included some reflections of our own regarding Larry's next step.

Larry has several options for incorporating his analysis of his students' methods and
representations into his next lesson. He could emphasize their different approaches by
creating a poster that shows the four main types of methods and to ask students to examine, discuss, and explain the methods (both their own and those of others). He could then
use that discussion to orchestrate a conversation that compares and contrasts the methods
and focuses on the mathematical relationships highlighted within each method. Another
option would be to ask various students to display their method on the blackboard or
whiteboard, being deliberate about the order in which students present their approaches.
For example, he might decide to begin with the visual methods, to go to the table next,
and to end with the recursive method. Or, depending on how many students used each
method, he may choose to share the method most students used first. He would make sure
that students not presenting were able to ask questions about the method. He might also
decide to ask random students to explain the method presented to assess whether they
understood another student's thinking. After discussing the various methods, Larry might
provide his students with another growth pattern and ask them to use a visual method and
a table method (or a recursive method and a visual method) to solve the problem. (Recall
that we saw the interviewer in Chapter 2 do something similar when she asked Kasage to
solve the addition problem using Julio's method.)

We hope that you, like Larry, will focus on careful examination and analysis of the
various methods (and representations) that emerge in your own classroom. Inevitably,
students will see problems differently than you (and than some of their peers), solving
them in ways that make sense to them. As teachers, we need to be able to recognize

the various solution methods and representations, figure out whether they accurately represent the content, and then decide how/if to use them in our lessons. This is mathematically challenging work that is unique to the work of teaching.

Your Own Practice and Work with Representations

In thinking about your own practice (individually or collectively with your colleagues), think about the following questions:

- What kinds of representations are most used in your curriculum materials? Are they used in ways that are accessible to students? Are there ways you might adapt them to better support student learning?

- Do you allow your students to select from multiple representations when working on math tasks? What representations do your students typically use? Are there some that they use more than others? Are there representations they do not use spontaneously but that you think might help them understand better?

- Can your students use representations to convey their thinking to others? Can they solve a problem using other students' representations and/or methods?

- Can your students move flexibly among different representations?

- What representations do you use with your students to help you teach specific concepts, such as fractions, multiplication, and so on?

Using Artifacts to Examine Representations in Your Classroom

Let's circle back to thinking about using artifacts from your classroom to examine the mathematical representations that you and your students use in solving problems. You might use common classroom artifacts to examine representations in your classroom.

Homework. Students solve problems in various ways, using a variety of representational forms to capture their thinking. Homework can provide a great window into how students use (or don't use) representations as tools for solving problems—especially when students are expected to show all their work and explain their reasoning. You can also use homework to get a sense of the types of representations your class as a whole is using. As in Larry's class, perhaps your students are using a few main types of representations. They might be different than the ones that you prefer. What do the representations your students use tell you about how they're thinking about the problem?

Warm-Ups. Warm-ups can be a nice, quick way to get a sense of your students' use of representations. Depending on the type of problem you choose, a warm-up might be used to elicit several different representations (e.g., physical objects, drawings, diagrams, tables, or algebraic notation) to get an idea of how comfortable students are with different ways of representing the mathematics. If time allows, help your students compare and contrast the different representations, looking at what each highlights about the mathematics. For example, you could examine a visual representation to see what relationships it emphasizes (such as "center and arms" or "number of minutes and number of dots added" from Exercise 1), or you could look at a table and a visual method to see how they highlight similar and different aspects of the problem.

Class Discussion. Problems posed as part of lessons, homework, or warm-ups can all serve to help fuel class discussions in which representations are linked to each other and to underlying mathematical ideas. You can ask students to write their solutions on the board or chart paper so that the class has visual access to the various methods and representations during the discussion.

Diagnostic Interviews. Diagnostic interviews can provide information about whether students are able to move flexibly among representations or whether their understanding is closely tied to a particular method. If a student gravitates to a one approach or representation, try using your interview to learn more about how that representation supports the student's thinking. Also try probing about what he or she finds confusing about other approaches or representations. This information can help you develop a more complete picture of the student's mathematical strengths and needs.

Wrapping Up

The goal of this chapter is to help you recognize that different methods for solving problems may highlight underlying mathematical ideas and perhaps deemphasize others. The more we are able to recognize the reasoning behind students' thinking—which often can be accessed by analyzing their representations—the better position we are in to help them connect to the big mathematical ideas and develop flexibility in moving among various representations. We hope that you'll take the opportunities we present in this chapter, including the additional exercises that follow, to practice honing your skills.

Additional Exercises

We end this chapter with additional exercises to support you as you practice analyzing representations. Exercise 2 is a video clip from an upper elementary fraction lesson, and Exercise 3 is a set of student representations from a third-grade geometry/measurement task involving area and perimeter. Each exercise includes study questions and a completed sample worksheet to help you with your reflections and discussion of the exercise.

Exercise 2: Video Games Fraction Lesson

In this video clip, the teacher poses a problem to her class about a student who has completed certain video game levels. She asks the students to decide which of three video games was closest to being completed:

- *Alien Attitude:* Two of the three levels completed
- *Basketball Boyz:* Three of the four levels completed
- *Dancing Divas:* Five of the eight levels completed

The students work in pairs to try to answer her question in as many ways as possible. The teacher provides the students with materials (cut-out circles and paper strips) and tells them that she will look for how they use these in solving the problem.

Process for Analyzing the Video Game Fractions Lesson Video. Follow the steps below as you complete this exercise. Read through all the steps before you begin in order to get an overview of the process.

PDToolkit
for
Examining Mathematics Practice through Classroom Artifacts

Step 1: Identify key math ideas. Think about the task and the key mathematical ideas it taps. Also predict some ways you think students might approach and represent the problem.

Step 2: Prepare to view the video. Make a copy of the blank Chapter 5 worksheet (located in the Appendix and as a writeable PDF on PDToolkit). Also have some scratch paper on hand for making notes about the representations the students use and their descriptions of their solution methods.

Step 3: Watch the *Video Games Fraction Lesson* video clip. Remember that you're viewing the video (found on PDToolkit) in order to describe and interpret the representations and solution methods the students use. Use the columns on the worksheet to help focus your viewing and jot down notes (and time codes) to support your analysis. You may want to view the clip once in its entirety and then review selected parts that seem particularly interesting or important to you.

Step 4: Complete the worksheet. Fill in the columns of the worksheet. Also note any questions or observations you might have about students' work.

Step 5: Reflect on your work. If you're working with others, take some time to discuss your analyses of the representations and of any possible connections you noted among them. Be sure to support your comments with evidence from the video. You might want to look over the completed sample worksheet to help you think about your own responses (see Table 5.2). Use the study questions as well to help you reflect on your observations (and, if you are working with others, to start your discussion).

Step 1: Identify key math ideas.

Step 2: Prepare to view the video.

Step 3: Watch the *Video Games Fraction Lesson* video clip.

Step 4: Complete the worksheet.

Step 5: Reflect on your work.

Study Questions

► How would you describe each of the representations to someone who hadn't seen the video?

► How are the representations similar? How are they different?

► What are the ways in which the representations highlight key ideas of the problem solution?

► What other representations might students have made?

► Think about the implications of the student work for teaching:

■ If you were the teacher of these students, how would you determine what students understood about fractions from their representations?

■ What additional representations might you encourage students to explore? Why?

■ What implications for your own teaching might you draw from this exercise?

The teacher challenged these students to use base-10 blocks to model the computations they performed when using the multiplication algorithm.

TABLE 5.2 Completed Sample Worksheet: *Video Games Fraction Lesson*

Mathematical Task (note the task and key mathematical ideas)	Representations/Approaches	Analysis and Connection of Representation
Video Games Completed A girl is in the process of playing three video games. She has completed some levels of each. What game is she closest to completing? Why? **Alien Attitude:** Two out of three levels completed **Basketball Boyz:** Three out of four levels completed **Dancing Divas:** Five out of eight levels completed Try to solve the problem in as many ways as possible. How did the materials help you to solve the problem? **Key Ideas:** • Fractions represent parts of a whole. • Comparing fractions requires a common reference whole. • Fractions are built out of unit fractions. • Fractions are numbers.	**Circles** Students fold cut-out circles into thirds, fourths, and eighths and shade in the appropriate number of levels completed for each game. 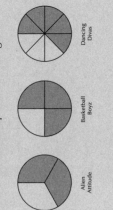 **Strips** Students fold strips of paper into thirds, fourths, and eighths, shading the levels completed for each game. 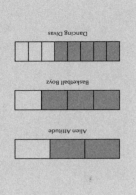	This method uses cut-out circles to make equal-sized sections. The number of sections in each circle correspond to the number of levels of each game: three for Alien Attitude, four for Basketball Boyz, and eight for Dancing Divas. Students shaded in the levels completed for each game on the appropriate circle. In students' presentations of their solution, they say what each shaded part/whole represents, but they do not say (nor were they asked) how completed portions compare across the three games or which game was closest to being completed. This method uses vertical strips of paper to make equal-sized sections. The number of sections also corresponds to the number of levels of each game. Students then shade (or label?) the levels completed for each game. In their presentations, they say what each shaded part/whole represents, but they do not say (nor were they asked) which game was closest to being completed. Questions: Will the teacher ask about which game was closest to completion later, after all groups have shared? Or does she assume that students know the answer because all the strips are the same length, so it is easy to see which one has the most shading? Or does she not ask because her focus is solely on representations and not on how the representations allow you to compare fractions? (This is only a small clip out of an entire lesson, so these questions might well be answered later.)

Continued

TABLE 5.2 Completed Sample Worksheet: *Video Games Fraction Lesson (continued)*

Mathematical Task (note the task and key mathematical ideas)	Representations/Approaches	Analysis and Connection of Representation
	Gustavo's Drawing	Gustavo divides each circle in his drawing into the equal sections, as did the other groups (three for Alien Attitude, four for Basketball Boyz, and eight for Dancing Divas). For each circle, he then labels each section as a fraction of the whole circle and continues around the circle counting and labeling sections (e.g., $\frac{1}{3}$, $\frac{2}{3}$, $\frac{3}{3}$). While this makes sense, the labels could create a problem—the section labeled $\frac{2}{3}$ is not two-thirds of the whole circle—it's the second one-third that he counts/labels. This way of representing the problem exists across all of his circles.
		Gustavo talks about how he compared fractions by placing them on top of each other so that he could see the shaded part and determine which one was closer to being finished. By stacking the representations, he has effectively created a common reference whole for comparing the games.
	Alien Attitude Basketball Boyz Dancing Divas	
	Another Possible Representation: The Number Line	This method doesn't appear on the video but is a possible alternative. It uses the number line as a representation for each of the games, using a line with an arrow to represent the completed levels. The three line segments are the same length to ensure that the wholes that are being compared are the same, and equivalent fractions are lined up.
	Alien Attitude Basketball Boyz Dancing Divas	

Exercise 3: Garden Border Task: Student Methods

107

Chapter 5
**Choosing,
Using, and
Connecting
Mathematical
Representations**

In this final exercise, you will examine a set of student representations from a third-grade geometry/measurement lesson. The problem focuses on the concept of area and perimeter. Ms. Alvarez asked her students to work on the Garden Border task (see Figure 5.11).

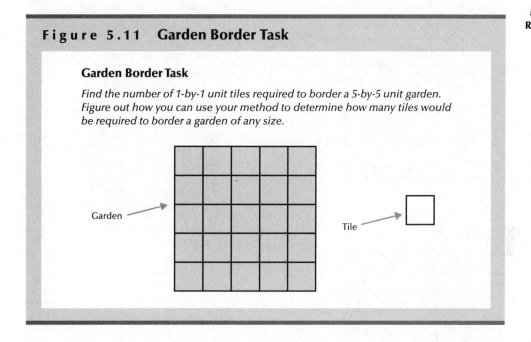

Figure 5.11   Garden Border Task

Garden Border Task

Find the number of 1-by-1 unit tiles required to border a 5-by-5 unit garden. Figure out how you can use your method to determine how many tiles would be required to border a garden of any size.

Garden

Tile

Students first worked individually and then in small groups to discuss their solutions and methods to the problem. Ms. Alvarez wasn't surprised that some students solved the problem successfully while others didn't, but she was amazed by the variety of methods and representations that her students used. She selected a representative sample of four of the most common approaches in order to analyze what her students did or did not understand (see Figure 5.12).

Process for Analyzing the Garden Border Work Samples. Follow the steps below as you complete this exercise. Read through all the steps before you begin in order to get an overview of the process.

Step 1:   Explore the Garden Border task. Do the problem for yourself to get a sense of how you think about (and represent) the task and then study the solutions in Figure 5.12. Did you use an approach that was similar to one of the four students' approaches? If so, try the remaining methods, too, in order to make sense out of them. If your way was different, try all four. Also think about the key mathematical ideas involved in this task.

Step 1:
Explore
the Garden
Border task.

F i g u r e 5.12   Garden Border Work Samples

Amy's Solution

You have 4 corners no matter how big the garden is. And you always have 4 sides to the garden border that have the same length as the garden itself—so you always have 4 sides + 4 corners.

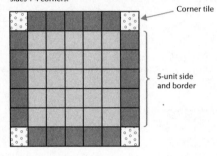

Corner tile

5-unit side and border

Mario's Solution

You have a top and bottom that have a side plus two corners each. And you have two sides that match the sides of the garden. Any garden will have a top and bottom, 2 sides + 2 corners each, and 2 more sides on either end.

Top is one side plus 2 corners

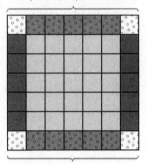

Bottom is one side plus 2 corners

Keisha's Solution

There are 4 groups of one corner and one side.

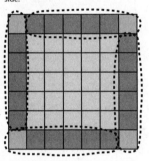

Zack's Solution

We cut out the garden from the border and counted the number of tiles left in the border and got 24 tiles. You can always cut out and count the leftovers.

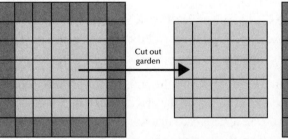

Cut out garden

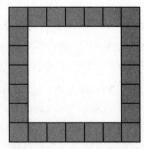

Step 2: **Complete the worksheet.** Make a copy of the blank Chapter 5 worksheet (located in the Appendix and as a writeable PDF on PDToolKit). Fill in the columns of the worksheet, noting any questions you have as well.

Step 3: **Reflect on your work.** If you're working with others, take some time to discuss your analyses of the representations and of any possible connections you noted among them. You might want to look over the completed sample worksheet to help you think about your own responses (see Table 5.3). Use the study questions as well to help you reflect on your observations (and, if you are working with others, to start your discussion).

Step 2:
Complete the worksheet.

Step 3:
Reflect on your work.

Study Questions

▶ How would you describe each of the solution methods and their representations?

▶ How are the four representations similar? How are they different?

▶ What are the strengths and limitations of each method?

▶ What other representations might students have made?

▶ Think about the implications of the student work for teaching:

  ▪ If you were Ms. Alvarez, what do the students' representations tell you about what they understand?

  ▪ What additional representations might you encourage students to explore?

  ▪ How did the use of various shades of gray help students represent the problem solution? How might color be used?

  ▪ What implications for your own teaching might you draw from this exercise?

TABLE 5.3 Completed Sample Worksheet: Garden Border

Mathematical Task (note the task and key mathematical ideas)	Representations/Approaches	Analysis and Connection of Representations
Garden Border Task Find the number of one-by-one unit tiles required to border a five-by-five unit garden. Figure out how you can use your method to determine how many tiles would be required to border a garden of any size. 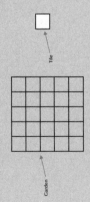 **Key Ideas:** • The situation can be seen as a dynamic growing configuration. In this case, four tiles are needed each time the garden grows by one linear unit. • There are a number of different yet equivalent approaches to solving the problem. • You can reason about the general case by thinking about specific examples. • Connection to later study of algebra: the relationship between the number of tiles needed and the dimension of the garden is a linear function.	**Amy's Solution** *You have four corners no matter how big the garden is. And you always have four sides to the garden border that have the same length as the garden itself—so you always have four sides + four corners.* 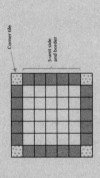 **Mario's Solution** *You have a top and bottom that have a side plus two corners each. And you have two sides that match the sides of the garden. Any garden will have a top and a bottom, two sides + two corners each and two more sides on either end.* 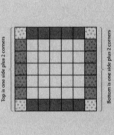	Amy visualizes the border as two distinct parts: (1) the four corners (patterned white squares) and (2) the four dark gray sides that correspond to the sides of the square garden. She uses the pattern and the gray to represent the two distinct parts of the border. These may have helped her visualize that the border of any garden always consists of four corners and four sides and that the length of the border sides are equal to the length of the garden sides. Mario visualizes the border as tops and bottoms that are equal in length—they each have a side that corresponds to the garden side in units—and each also includes two corners. Mario uses patterned gray for the sides and patterned white for the corners. Top and bottom each have one side and two corners, so together, there are two sides and four corners (or one side + two corners + one side + two corners). He represents the remaining part of the border—the two vertical sides—with dark gray and notices that the total number of side squares corresponds to the side length. This method is similar to Amy's in that both methods distinguish four corners and recognize that the sides of the border are equal in the number of units to the corresponding side of the garden bed.

Continued

TABLE 5.2 Completed Sample Worksheet: Garden Border (*continued*)

Mathematical Task (note the task and key mathematical ideas)	Representations/Approaches	Analysis and Connection of Representations
	Keisha's Solution *There are four groups made of one corner and one side. These groups wrap around the garden.* 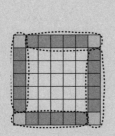	Keisha breaks the border into four distinct and equal parts—one side + one corner. She wraps around the garden as she represents her groupings (dark gray for sides and light gray for the corners), using a dotted line to circle each group. Like Amy's and Mario's methods, Keisha distinguishes between the sides and the corners. Her solution most closely resembles Amy's in that she sees the border in two distinct parts: the corners and the sides. The two representations differ in how they count those parts: Amy counts the four corners and the four sides, and Keisha counts one side + one corner four times.
	Zack's Solution *We cut out the garden from the border and counted the number of tiles left in the border and got 24 tiles. You can always cut out and count the leftovers.* 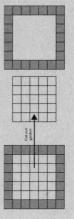	Zack looked at the problem in a holistic way. He saw the entire border separate from the garden and used color to distinguish them—dark gray for the border and light gray for the garden. He then "cut" the garden out so that he was left with only the border and counted the tiles to find his solution. He mentions that you can use this method for any garden. Zack's method can be generalized for any size garden and border (though probably not by third graders). The entire structure—garden and border—has dimensions (n + 2) by (n + 2), where n = side length of the garden. The area of the entire structure has an area of $(n + 2)^2$, while the area of the garden alone is n^2. The difference of the two areas gives the area of the border alone: $(n + 2)^2 - n^2$.

111

Section 3

Putting It All Together in the Classroom

Skillful Use of Artifacts Framework	
SKILLFUL USE OF ARTIFACTS INVOLVES:	
Attention to Thinking	**Attention to Content**
▶ distinguish between description and interpretation of work represented in artifacts	▶ use a guiding mathematical framework to discuss the mathematical content in artifacts
▶ ground interpretations of thinking in evidence from artifacts	▶ compare/contrast different representations of mathematical ideas captured in artifacts
▶ generate plausible alternative interpretations of thinking and justify ideas with evidence	▶ compare/contrast mathematical explanations and solution methods represented in artifacts
▶ see strengths (not just weaknesses) in thinking and understanding captured in artifacts	▶ use the exploration of mathematics to develop/engage norms of mathematical argument

Source: Adapted from Nikula, J., Goldsmith, L. T., Blasi, Z. V., & Seago, N. (2006). A framework for the strategic use of classroom artifacts in mathematics professional development. *NCSM Journal, 9*(1), 59.

We started this book by emphasizing the importance of developing a vision of mathematics instruction that had multiple lenses. In subsequent chapters, we've considered classroom artifacts from a variety of perspectives. We've focused on using them to describe and interpret students' thinking, to examine student errors and consider ways to use errors to build deeper understanding, to apply guiding mathematical frameworks in the analysis of curriculum materials, and to explore how students' use of different representations in problem solving can illuminate different aspects of the mathematics.

We've utilized the Skillful Use of Artifacts framework to articulate our approaches to analyzing artifacts from the classroom. The framework emphasizes our experience that skillful work with artifacts requires attention to both thinking and content.

The two main sections of this book mirror the two components of the framework—*attention to thinking* and *attention to content*—and individual chapters have highlighted different bulleted points in the framework. Throughout these chapters, we've worked with artifacts that capture small slices of lessons in order to practice using different lenses for viewing math learning and teaching. We've used these slices to look at different facets of professional vision—descriptions and interpretations of student thinking, the reasoning behind students' errors, the big ideas that underlie particular mathematical content, the practices and habits of mind that facilitate mathematical work, and different ways of representing mathematical tasks and solution methods. Because our focus has been on inquiring into students' thinking rather than on intervening to change it, we've encouraged you to set aside your judgments about what teachers *should* or *might* have done to advance students' understanding as you've worked with the artifacts in this book.

In our final chapter, we put all the facets together, applying these different ways of focusing work with artifacts to an entire lesson. Our goal in this final chapter is to integrate these multiple perspectives to consider how the information we glean from our artifact analysis can inform instruction.

6

Putting It All Together

Lately, Jeffrey Stockdale has been prospecting in his fifth-grade math class. He started panning for information about students' understanding with some of his homework assignments. He still starts each lesson having students trade papers and check answers and still asks students if there are any parts of the assignment that really gave them trouble, but his real work with the homework happens after class. Instead of just checking off assignments for completeness and recording scores, he's started looking more closely at students' errors. He's been particularly focused on identifying common mistakes that seem to suggest something's "off" in students' reasoning, and he's begun to use this information to plan ways to strengthen their understanding. If lots of students seemed to be having trouble, he'll use his analysis to plan additional lessons; if only a few students seemed to be having issues, he'd look for time to work with them individually.

He's also started talking with the three other fifth-grade teachers at their planning meetings, discussing with them some of the thinking he'd been observing in class. They'd been trading stories for years about the places their students got tripped up, but now they've all started digging a little deeper into why this might be happening. They've also been spending some time exchanging ideas about activities and approaches specifically focused on boosting students' understanding rather than just sharing fun activities that engaged their students.

Since we met Jeffrey in Chapter 1, he's staked a claim on his gold mine. He (and his colleagues as well) have discovered that they feel more successful in their teaching when they use analyses of what their students do—and don't—currently understand to drive their instructional decisions. By attending carefully to students' thinking, Jeffrey and his colleagues are better able to put themselves in their students' conceptual shoes and to make stronger connections between the kids' current understanding and the mathematical ideas and skills they are teaching. They are becoming more deliberate about considering both the underlying mathematical content of their lessons and the ways that students' work reveals their understanding of the content. The teachers are also beginning to see the importance of planning lessons that include opportunities to gather information about students' thinking.

Jeffrey started to open the window on his students' thinking slowly, taking a more careful look at one small part of his teaching—his students' homework. In the previous chapters, we've also worked on opening windows into students' thinking by working on artifacts that highlight slices of lessons—investigating students' written work, viewing a short segment of class discussion, and analyzing curriculum materials. We end the book by putting all of these pieces together as we work with an entire lesson.

Exercises: Integrated Analysis of Whole Lessons

We're going to work on two lessons in this chapter, a sixth-grade geometry lesson and a fourth-grade lesson on multidigit multiplication. To get an overview of each lesson, we actually have a new kind of artifact for you—lesson graphs we built by reviewing the video records of each class. Nanette invented the lesson graph about 10 years ago to summarize videotaped lessons from the TIMSS 1999 Video Study. This study included publicly released videos documenting typical mathematics lessons in seven countries, lesson graphs for each video lesson, copies of textbook pages, and examples of worksheets and student work samples (Hiebert, Gallimore, Garnier et al., 2003). Since then, she's used them in several other video-based professional development programs (Seago, Driscoll, Callahan et al., in press; Seago, Mumme, & Branca, 2004).

A lesson graph captures the flow of activities within the lesson and highlights mathematically important and/or interesting moments in class. It's a one-page summary that represents the proportion of time allotted to different parts of the lesson and concisely maps the mathematical arc of students' work as they engage with the mathematical task(s), their classmates, and their teacher over the course of the lesson. It provides a context for analysis of video segments like the ones we used in Chapter 3 and is also useful for considering how ideas interconnect and build over the course of the lesson.

116

Section 3

**Putting It
All Together
in the
Classroom**

We'll use the lesson graph here to get a sense of the lesson as a whole and to see how the different facets we've explored individually in earlier chapters unfold within a lesson. Figure 6.1 is a sample lesson graph that comes from a class that used the "Growing Dots" problem you worked with in Chapter 5.

Like this sample, the lesson graphs we'll use are divided into separate sections for each segment of the lesson. Gray sections of the lesson graph denote students'

F i g u r e   6 . 1   Sample lesson graph

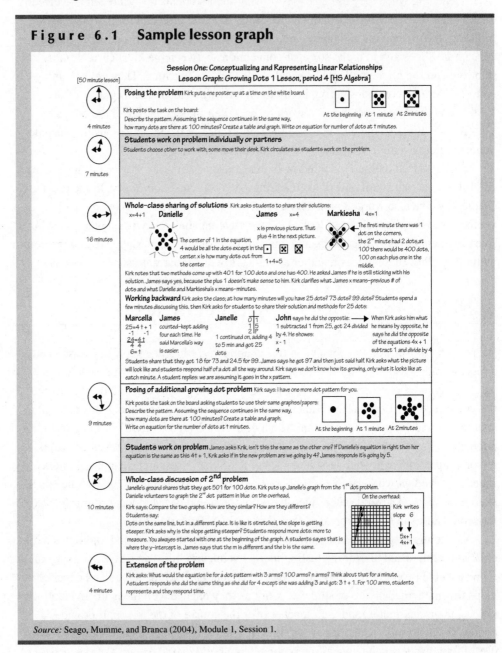

Source: Seago, Mumme, and Branca (2004), Module 1, Session 1.

independent work (the teacher may "float" but does not control the work flow), and white sections indicate when students are working as a whole class. The height of the sections is proportionate to the amount of time the activity took during class: the less time spent on the activity, the shorter the section. For example, a 25-minute activity is five times as tall as a five-minute activity. The lesson graphs for the two lessons in this chapter note time codes for each activity as well as each subactivity on the left-hand side of the graph. The time codes will help you to identify video segments you'd like to watch to clarify or elaborate on the information in the lesson graph or to view segments that interest or puzzle you. In addition, videos of both lessons are available on PDToolKit. We don't expect you to watch it in its entirety (unless you'd like to); rather, you should select short clips to investigate, much like we've done for you in earlier chapters. The purpose of these exercises is to integrate the different perspectives we've taken into a single analysis of students' mathematical thinking as a lesson unfolds.

Exercise 1: *Building Triangles* Lesson

The lesson in this exercise comes from the sixth-grade *Shapes and Designs* unit of the *Connected Mathematics* curriculum (Lappan, Fey, Fitzgerald, Friel, & Phillips, 1998). The unit as a whole focuses on understanding properties of shapes by engaging students in a series of explorations of angles and side lengths of polygons. The *Building Triangles* lesson kicks off a five-day investigation of properties relating to the side lengths of different kinds of polygons. The 45-minute class on the video consisted of three activities: (1) the teacher's launch of the problem, (2) pair/small-group work on the task, and (3) whole-class discussion of students' findings.

Process for Viewing and Analyzing the *Building Triangles* Lesson. Follow the steps below to complete the exercise. Read through all the steps before you begin in order to get an overview of the process.

PDToolKit
for
*Examining Mathematics
Practice through
Classroom Artifacts*

Step 1: **Examine the lesson graph and study the math task.** Read over the lesson graph for *Building Triangles* (see Figure 6.2) to get a sense of how the lesson unfolds. Study the math task and think about how students might approach it. What are the important ideas you would want students to take away from this lesson? Mark any places in the lesson graph that you feel might need clarification or more context.

Step 1: Examine the lesson graph and study the math task.

Step 2: **Prepare to watch the video.** Make a copy of the blank Chapter 6 Worksheet (see Figure 6.3), which is located in the Appendix and as a writeable PDF on PDToolKit. Get some scratch paper for jotting down notes as you watch the video. You may also want to make a copy of the lesson graph.

Step 2: Prepare to watch the video.

Figure 6.2 *Building Triangles* **lesson graph**

Building Triangles: A Sixth-Grade Lesson

00:00 – 07:08 [~7 minutes]	**Launching the lesson** Teacher asks students to recall the previous lesson on polygons. She says that they will work today with 3-sided polygons (triangles), using polystrips. She reviews how to use them, building a triangle with side lengths 6 units, 8 units, 12 units. Teacher: "Here's my question. Do you think any 3 numbers will create a triangle?" Some students say yes, some students say no, others are unsure. Task: Roll three number cubes. Find the sum of the numbers. Record this as the length of side 1. Roll the number cubes again and find the sum. This is side 2. Do the same for side 3. Try to build a triangle with these three numbers. Record whether or not you are able to create a triangle and draw a sketch of it. Use the group poster to record your findings.
07:09 – 27:02 [~20 minutes]	**Students work in pairs/small groups** Teacher passes out chart paper to each group with preset columns: Each group has: • Number cubes in a cup • Brads • Polystrips • Marker

Side 1	Side 2	Side 3	Triangle?	Sketch

13:06 – 15:53	▶ Student creates a triangle that doesn't work (10, 5, 18) T: "Do you think if you try again with the same numbers it will work?" Ss: "Yes." Students try using 18 first, then 5, and 10. Then they try first joining the sides measuring 5 and 10, and then joining the side measuring 18. They giggle at the "triangle" they create. They end up filling in "no" in the "Triangle?" column.
15:53 – 16:06	▶ Jamie draws a representation of what the 3-sided polystrip looked like to convey that the polystrip bent. He says it looks like an ice cream scoop.
22:00 – 22:24	▶ Student traces the triangle her group just made. Her partner tells her to write in the numbers inside the triangle.
24:55 – 27:02	▶ Another student makes the beginnings of a conjecture—he looks across the columns at the lengths of sides and says, "If it's a high number to a low number to a lower number [i.e., side 1-side 2-side 3], it won't work." He adds that "it might work if it is a high number, high number, low number."
27:23 – 45:02 [~18 minutes]	**Whole-class discussion** Teacher puts up all of the groups' charts, noting that two groups had measurements that didn't make triangles. She starts the discussion with a set of side lengths that didn't make a triangle (10, 5, 18). Megan: It had all high numbers and one low number. Maybe that is why it didn't work, because 18 is the highest number you can get; we had trouble with the sides of that 18 size. Teacher: Which side did you start with? Megan: 10, then 5, then 18 (18 on the bottom), then we started over again. Jaime: It didn't work, then we tried 18, 5, 10 and it still didn't work; we tried 5, 10, 18 and it still didn't work. Nicole: 10 + 5 + 18 = 33. We added 14, 6, and 12 = 32. We think that if you go past 32, it might not work. Jaime: 34 worked. Nichole: Or maybe 18 doesn't work—if you have 18 as a side, it won't work. Michael: I don't think that's right because what if you had three 18's instead of just one? Teacher: See if you can build one real quickly at your table?
31:57 – 33:32	▶ *Students work on creating an 18, 18, 18 triangle. Jaime says it works because all sides are equal and that's an equilateral triangle.* Teacher holds up an 18, 18, 18 triangle and asks if this disproves the theory that 18 as a side won't work. Loretta: I think it's not working because the other sides are going to be smaller than the 18. They'll be a little short so you'll have to bend it. Teacher points to another group's chart where a triplet doesn't work (17, 4, 9) and asks how it relates to what Loretta said.
35:49 – 37:26	▶ Jaime: You have to exceed the higher number. If the two other numbers add up, it might not work—it has to be higher than that. Teacher revoices Jamie's conjecture and says "Let's see if that happened to all of our numbers."
39:16 – 40:26	▶ Megan: If you have two numbers that are higher than the last number, they can stretch (and reach). S: It's actually the two lowest numbers. If they add up to be higher then the highest number, it will work. Megan: If you ever have 3 numbers and the 2 lowest added together are higher than the 3rd, then you don't have to draw a triangle.
41:32 – 43:13	▶ Teacher: "One more thing I want to talk about today and it happened in this group. When they got to the triangle that didn't work, they tried it again using a different order." She uses a polystrip triangle to demonstrate a rotation, shifting the placement of the sides and asks, "Does this triangle look different than the 1st one?"
44:06 – 45:07	▶ Teacher ends the lesson by telling the students that they will be exploring quadrilaterals tomorrow. She says, "Two people are absent today. Can you tell me what you will tell them tomorrow in a clear statement; how you can tell if three numbers will make a triangle?" A student makes a statement.

F i g u r e   6 . 3   Blank Chapter 6 worksheet

Chapter 6 Worksheet: Integrated Analysis of a Lesson

Lesson:

*Use evidence from the lesson graph and selective video viewings to back up your analysis.

Activity Description	Key Mathematical Idea(s)	Key Mathematical Practices/Habits of Mind	Key Mathematical Representations	Student Thinking	Errors/Incomplete Thinking; Questions re: Thinking
Activity 1:					
Activity 2:					
Activity 3:					
Activity 4:					

Copyright © Pearson Education

Step 3: **Choose video segments to watch.** Identify and watch any segments of the *Building Triangles* video (found on PDToolkit) that you think will help clarify or elaborate on the lesson graph. You can use the lesson graph time codes to help you locate the segments. If you'd *like* to view the whole lesson, feel free to do so—however, we imagine that you will use the lesson graph to get an overall sense of the lesson and to help you identify a limited number of places in the video to examine more fully.

Step 4: **Complete the Chapter 6 worksheet.** Be as specific with your observations and analyses as possible. Make sure that you've used evidence from the lesson graph and your video viewing to support your claims on the worksheet, for example, specific time codes for events, direct quotations of student's comments, and/or particular representations (either from the lesson graph summary or the video itself).

Step 5: **Reflect on your work.** If you're working with others, take some time to discuss your observations and analysis of the lesson. Be sure to support your comments with evidence from the video. You might want to look over the completed sample worksheet (Table 6.1) to help you think about your own responses. Use the study questions as well to help you reflect on your observations (and, if you are working with others, to start your discussion).

Step 3:
Choose video segments to watch.

Step 4:
Complete the Chapter 6 worksheet.

Step 5:
Reflect on your work.

120

Section 3

**Putting It
All Together
in the
Classroom**

Study Questions

▶ What are the key math ideas and skills in this lesson? What kinds of experiences during the lesson promoted students' work on these ideas and skills?

▶ What mathematical practices and/or habits of mind did students display?

▶ What representations did students use? How did the different representations relate to the key math content of the lesson?

▶ Did you identify any errors or incomplete understanding during this lesson? If so, what interpretations do you have about the reasoning that might have led to them?

▶ How did the students' ideas develop over the course of the lesson?

▶ What questions about students' understanding might you have pursued had this been your class?

Classroom artifacts can help teachers follow students' thinking and connect it to important mathematical ideas and skills.

TABLE 6.1 Completed Sample Worksheet: *Building Triangles Lesson*

Activity Description	Key Mathematical Idea(s)	Key Mathematical Practices/Habits of Mind	Key Mathematical Representations	Student Thinking	Errors/Incomplete Thinking; Questions re: Thinking
Activity 1: Launching the lesson	• Characteristics of a triangle: Teacher's question—do any three numbers create a triangle? [00:00–07:08].	• Use current knowledge to reflect on question. • Use tools/models strategically (polystrips)	• Polystrips to build triangles [00:00–07:08]	• Nothing significant to observe	• None
Activity 2: Students work in pairs/small groups to explore lengths that create triangles	• Triangle inequality theorem: sum of two shorter sides must be greater than the longest side • Only one unique triangle can be made with a given set of side lengths • Triangles with the same side lengths are congruent	• Make sense of problem and persevere in solving it [13:06] • Reason abstractly [13:06, 15:53, 24:55] • Construct viable arguments and critique the reasoning of others [24:55] • Use appropriate tools strategically [7:09] • Look for structure • Communicate thinking [24:55]	• Students use physical models to build and trace triangles (polystrips in each group) [22:00] • Students examine numerical relationships [24:55] • Students use table to organize data [24:55] • Jaime represents a nontriangle as an ice cream scoop [15:53]	• Some combinations of side sizes will not produce a triangle [13:06] • The relationship among the sides is important—if the sum of two side lengths isn't greater than the length of the third side, you can't make a flat figure [Jaime's "scoop" 15:530] • Students' understanding was evidenced in their ability to justify their reasoning [Students in small group at 13:06, Jaime 15:53]	• One group writes values of side lengths inside triangles in a way that seems disconnected to the sides themselves [22:00] • Students were looking for patterns and/or regularities in places that prove to be unproductive [24:55]
Activity 3: Whole-class discussion of observations	• Same as Activity 2	• Reason abstractly • Construct viable arguments and critique the reasoning of others • Use appropriate tools strategically • Look for structure • Communicate thinking	• Students use tables to represent data [group posters] • Students build 18, 18, 18 triangles with polystrips (physical model); teacher holds up a polystrip triangle to prove 18 works [33:32]	• There are special triangles [Michael 31:00+; Jaime 33:32] • Student understanding was evidenced in their ability to justify their reasoning [Jaime, Megan, Nicole, Michael, Loretta]	• Nicole reasoned about specific values of particular triangles rather than thinking relationally [31:00+] • Megan thinks that 18 doesn't work • Some students might have believed that the order of joining the sides changed the triangle [44:06]

* Use evidence from the lesson graph and selective video viewings to back up your analysis

122

Section 3
**Putting It
All Together
in the
Classroom**

Commentary on the *Building Triangles* Lesson. In the *Building Triangles* lesson we can see elements of each of the five lenses we've highlighted in this book and included in the Chapter 6 worksheet.

- Students working on a mathematical task that provides them opportunities to encounter *important math ideas*
- Students engaging in *mathematical practices/habits of mind*
- Students using *mathematical representations* to help them reason
- Students sharing and revising their *thinking*
- Students' *erroneous or incomplete thinking*

The following aspects of the lesson were salient to us as we considered these lenses.

This lesson was a cognitively demanding one. It focused on both important *mathematical ideas* and *mathematical practices/habits of mind*, engaging students in an exploration of side lengths for the purpose of learning an important property of triangles. By examining their data and reasoning conceptually, the class developed conjectures related to the Triangle Inequality Theorem—that the sum of the lengths of any two sides of a triangle must be greater than the length of the third. It's also noteworthy that the teacher set up the lesson such that the group discussion was critical. Two of the groups rolled triplets that were all possible to construct and therefore had no data of their own that would help them conjecture about the conditions that would—and wouldn't—create a triangle. Furthermore, it was through their discussions with each other that students shaped conjectures and arguments that accounted for their data in a convincing way.

The polystrip exploration engaged a number of *mathematical practices and habits of mind*. Students worked with others to model mathematical situations, make observations and reason from them, propose conjectures, test their ideas, and revise their thinking. They also examined other students' ideas and responded in mathematically principled ways. For example, in the exchange between Jaime, Nicole, and Michael (captured at the beginning of the *Whole-Class Discussion* section of the lesson graph and around time code 27:23 in the video), Nicole described her group's work and tentative conclusions ("$10 + 5 + 18 = 33$; we added 14, 6, and $12 = 32$. We think that if you go past 32 it might not work"), and Jamie challenged them using data from his group, noting that 34 worked. Michael also disagreed with Nicole but from a more conceptually based position, implying that their thinking was incorrect because equilateral triangles have sides of the same length and therefore that it's possible to make a triangle with each side measuring 18 ("I don't think that is right because what if you had three 18s instead of just one?").

Over the course of the lesson, students refined their thinking about the question their teacher posed ("Do you think any three numbers will create a triangle?"). They moved from a general observation about combinations of "low" and "high" numbers to Loretta's conjecture about three-quarters of the way through the class that if two sides of the triangle together are shorter than the third side, they'll be too short and you will have to "bend it" (31:57).

In keeping with the *Principals and Standards* of the National Council of Teachers of Mathematics (2000) and the Common Core State Standards (2010), in this lesson students used various types of *representations* to help them explore and reason about the teacher's question. These representations served somewhat different purposes over the course of the lesson.

- The polystrips allowed students to easily and accurately build triangles with side lengths determined by the numbers they rolled with the number cubes. The accuracy was particularly important for helping them make observations, formulate and test conjectures, and make mathematical generalizations about the side lengths.

- Students also used these physical models to describe and justify their reasoning; for example, Jaime's comments (at 35:49) about the third side having to measure more than the sum of the other two sides.

- Students used quantitative representations of triangles to describe and reason about relationships among the sides; for example, students referred to side lengths and their sums throughout much of the lesson.

- Students took advantage of multiple representations to support their reasoning. Many students moved back and forth between physical models and numeric representations to represent, test, and refine conjectures.

There was also some evidence of *incorrect or incomplete understanding* during the lesson. Several of the students' ideas struck us as noteworthy.

- The order in which the sides are joined affects the ability to create a triangle. Students didn't trust their results when they got a triangle that didn't work and tried changing the order in which they connected the sides to see if that would make a difference (13:06, 27:03). It's possible that the students were thinking that a 10, 5, 18 triangle is different from an 18, 10, 5 triangle. It is also possible that the students believed that all side lengths had to work since a triangle has three sides.

- The absolute size of a side determines whether you can make a triangle, regardless of the sizes of the other sides. Some students reasoned about specific values of particular triangles rather than thinking relationally (e.g., Nicole at ~31:00[+]).

- The relationship between numeric and diagrammatic representations may not be clear for students. One group writes values of side lengths inside triangles in a way that seems disconnected to the sides themselves (22:00).

Some Additional Points of Reflection. Before we move on to Exercise 2, take a few more minutes to reflect on what it was like to review the lesson graph and view this video while keeping several perspectives going simultaneously.

124

Section 3
**Putting It
All Together
in the
Classroom**

- Were both of the artifacts—lesson graph and video—useful to you? How did you use them?
- Were you able to analyze and provide evidence for all five perspectives represented by the columns in the worksheet?
- Did some of these perspectives feel more useful than others in terms of thinking about students' learning?
- How was what you noticed similar and different from what your colleagues (or what we) noticed? Did you find things that we didn't take note of?

Exercise 2: *Multiplication* Lesson

This second exercise focuses on a slightly younger group of children—fourth graders— and addresses a different curricular strand—number and operation. The lesson centers on multidigit multiplication, which is a topic that can be approached from a conceptual standpoint or from a more rote/procedural one.

We don't have information about the origins of this lesson; it may have come from a published math program, or it may have been a problem that the teacher, Mr. Martinez, created on his own for his class. The 80-minute lesson consisted of four activities: (1) warm-ups (both mental math and journal problems), (2) the teacher's lesson launch, (3) small-group work on the problem, and (4) whole-class discussion.

The lesson graph (Figure 6.4) follows the same design as the *Building Triangles* lesson. It's divided proportionally into the four different activities and provides time codes as support for viewing particular segments of the lesson that we thought were noteworthy. You'll be following the same process for analyzing the lesson as you did in Exercise 1.

Process for Viewing and Analyzing the *Multiplication* Lesson. Follow the steps below to complete the exercise. Read through all the steps before you begin in order to get an overview of the process.

Step 1: Examine the lesson graph and study the math task.

Step 1: Examine the lesson graph and study the math task. Read over the lesson graph for Mr. Martinez's *Multiplication* lesson to get a sense of how it unfolds. Study the math tasks and think about how students might approach them. What are the important ideas you would want students to take away from this lesson? Mark any places in the lesson graph that you feel might need clarification or more context.

Step 2: Prepare to watch the video.

Step 2: Prepare to watch the video. Make a copy of the blank Chapter 6 Worksheet (located in the Appendix and as a writeable PDF on PDToolKit). Have scratch paper handy and make a copy of the lesson graph.

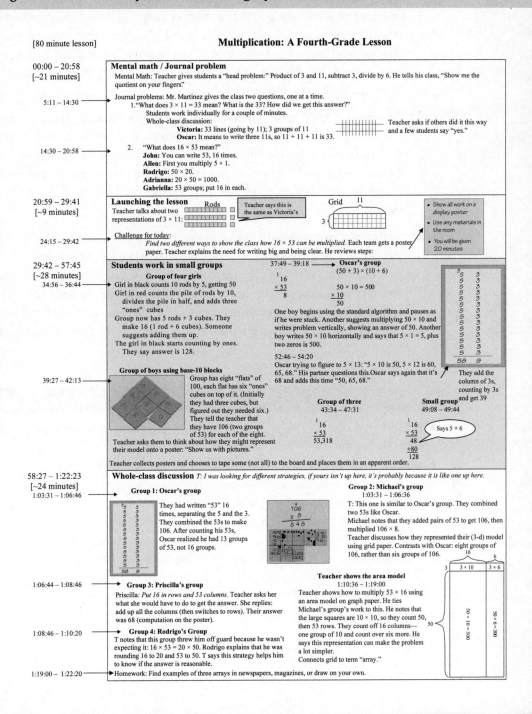

Multiplication: A Fourth-Grade Lesson

[80 minute lesson]

00:00 – 20:58
[~21 minutes]

Mental math / Journal problem

Mental Math: Teacher gives students a "head problem:" Product of 3 and 11, subtract 3, divide by 6. He tells his class, "Show me the quotient on your fingers."

5:11 – 14:30

Journal problems: Mr. Martinez gives the class two questions, one at a time.
1. "What does 3 × 11 = 33 mean? What is the 33? How did we get this answer?"
   Students work individually for a couple of minutes.
   Whole-class discussion:
   Victoria: 33 lines (going by 11); 3 groups of 11
   Oscar: It means to write three 11s, so 11 + 11 + 11 is 33.
   Teacher asks if others did it this way and a few students say "yes."

14:30 – 20:58

2. "What does 16 × 53 mean?"
   John: You can write 53, 16 times.
   Allen: First you multiply 5 × 1.
   Rodrigo: 50 × 20.
   Adrianna: 20 × 50 = 1000.
   Gabriella: 53 groups; put 16 in each.

20:59 – 29:41
[~9 minutes]

Launching the lesson

Teacher talks about two representations of 3 × 11:   Rods   Teacher says this is the same as Victoria's   Grid 11

- Show all work on a display poster
- Use any materials in the room
- You will be given 20 minutes

24:15 – 29:42

Challenge for today:
Find two different ways to show the class how 16 × 53 can be multiplied. Each team gets a poster paper. Teacher explains the need for writing big and being clear. He reviews steps:

29:42 – 57:45
[~28 minutes]

Students work in small groups

34:56 – 36:44

Group of four girls
Girl in black counts 10 rods by 5, getting 50
Girl in red counts the pile of rods by 10, divides the pile in half, and adds three "ones" cubes
Group now has 5 rods + 3 cubes. They make 16 (1 rod + 6 cubes). Someone suggests adding them up.
The girl in black starts counting by ones. They say answer is 128.

37:49 – 39:18   **Oscar's group**
(50 + 3) × (10 + 6)

$$\begin{array}{r} 1 \\ 16 \\ \times\ 53 \\ \hline 8 \end{array}$$

50 × 10 = 500
× 10
50

One boy begins using the standard algorithm and pauses as if he were stuck. Another suggests multiplying 50 × 10 and writes problem vertically, showing an answer of 50. Another boy writes 50 × 10 horizontally and says that 5 × 1 = 5, plus two zeros is 500.

52:46 – 54:20
Oscar trying to figure to 5 × 13: "5 × 10 is 50, 5 × 12 is 60, 65, 68." His partner questions this. Oscar says again that it's 68 and adds this time "50, 65, 68."

5   3
5   3
5   3
5   3
5   3
5   3
5   3
5   3
5   3
5   3
5   3
5   3
5   3
58   9

They add the column of 3s, counting by 3s, and get 39

39:27 – 42:13

Group of boys using base-10 blocks
Group has eight "flats" of 100, each flat has six "ones" cubes on top of it. (Initially they had three cubes, but figured out they needed six.) They tell the teacher that they have 106 (two groups of 53) for each of the eight.
Teacher asks them to think about how they might represent their model onto a poster: "Show us with pictures."

Group of three
43:34 – 47:31

$$\begin{array}{r} 1 \\ 16 \\ \times\ 53 \\ \hline 53,318 \end{array}$$

Small group
49:08 – 49:44

$$\begin{array}{r} 1 \\ 16 \\ \times\ 53 \\ \hline 48 \\ +80 \\ \hline 128 \end{array}$$

Says 5 × 6

Teacher collects posters and chooses to tape some (not all) to the board and places them in an apparent order.

58:27 – 1:22:23
[~24 minutes]

Whole-class discussion *T: I was looking for different strategies, if yours isn't up here, it's probably because it is like one up here.*

1:03:31 – 1:06:46

Group 1: Oscar's group

5   3
5   3
5   3
5   3
5   3
5   3
5   3
5   3
5   3
5   3
5   3
58   9

They had written "53" 16 times, separating the 5 and the 3. They combined the 53s to make 106. After counting his 53s, Oscar realized he had 13 groups of 53, not 16 groups.

Group 2: Michael's group
1:03:31 – 1:06:36

$$\begin{array}{r} 4 \\ 106 \\ \times\ 8 \\ \hline 848 \end{array}$$

T: This one is similar to Oscar's group. They combined two 53s like Oscar.
Michael notes that they added pairs of 53 to get 106, then multiplied 106 × 8.
Teacher discusses how they represented their (3-d) model using grid paper. Contrasts with Oscar: eight groups of 106, rather than six groups of 106.

Teacher shows the area model
1:10:36 – 1:19:00
Teacher shows how to multiply 53 × 16 using an area model on graph paper. He ties Michael's group's work to this. He notes that the large squares are 10 × 10, so they count 50, then 53 rows. They count off 16 columns— one group of 10 and count over six more. He says this representation can make the problem a lot simpler.
Connects grid to term "array."

	10	6
3	3 × 10	3 × 6
50	50 × 10 = 500	50 × 6 = 300

1:06:44 – 1:08:46

Group 3: Priscilla's group
Priscilla: *Put 16 in rows and 53 columns.* Teacher asks her what she would have to do to get the answer. She replies: add up all the columns (then switches to rows). Their answer was 68 (computation on the poster).

1:08:46 – 1:10:20

Group 4: Rodrigo's Group
T notes that this group threw him off guard because he wasn't expecting it: 16 × 53 = 20 × 50. Rodrigo explains that he was rounding 16 to 20 and 53 to 50. T says this strategy helps him to know if the answer is reasonable.

1:19:00 – 1:22:20
Homework: Find examples of three arrays in newspapers, magazines, or draw on your own.

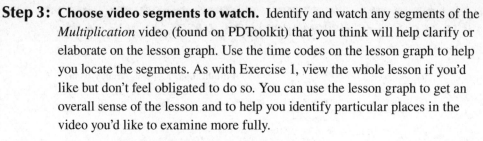

Step 3:
Choose video segments to watch.

Step 4:
Complete the worksheet.

Step 5:
Reflect on your work.

Step 3: Choose video segments to watch. Identify and watch any segments of the *Multiplication* video (found on PDToolkit) that you think will help clarify or elaborate on the lesson graph. Use the time codes on the lesson graph to help you locate the segments. As with Exercise 1, view the whole lesson if you'd like but don't feel obligated to do so. You can use the lesson graph to get an overall sense of the lesson and to help you identify particular places in the video you'd like to examine more fully.

Step 4: Complete the Chapter 6 worksheet. Be as specific with your observations and analyses as possible. Make sure that you've used evidence from the lesson graph and your video viewing to support your claims on the worksheet, for example, specific time codes for events, direct quotations of students' comments, and/or particular representations (either from the lesson graph summary or from the video itself).

Step 5: Reflect on your work. If you're working with others, take some time to discuss your observations and analysis of the lesson. Be sure to support your comments with evidence from the video. You might want to look over the completed sample worksheet (Table 6.2) to help you think about your own responses. Use the study questions as well to help you reflect on your observations (and, if you are working with others, to start your discussion).

PDToolkit
for
Examining Mathematics Practice through Classroom Artifacts

Study Questions

▶ What are the key math ideas and skills in this lesson? What kinds of experiences during the lesson promoted students' work on these ideas and skills?

▶ How did the students' ideas develop over the course of the lesson?

▶ What mathematical practices and/or habits of mind did students display?

▶ What representations did students use? How did the different representations reflect students' ideas and support their thinking?

▶ Did you identify any errors or incomplete understanding during this lesson? If so, what interpretations do you have about the reasoning that might have led to them?

▶ How did the students' ideas develop over the course of the lesson?

▶ What questions about students' understanding might you have pursued had this been your class?

TABLE 6.2 Completed Sample Worksheet: *Multiplication Lesson*

Activity Description	Key Mathematical Idea(s)	Mathematical Practices/Habits of Mind	Mathematical Representations	Student Thinking	Errors/Incomplete Thinking; Questions re Thinking
Activity 1: "Head problem"/journal questions	• Arithmetic computation	• Attend to precision • Pay attention to the structure of the problem	• Victoria's grid shows 33 vertical lines in groups of 11 and 2 horizontal lines 	• Oscar: "it means three 11s so 11 + 11 + 11 is 33" • John: "you can write 53 16 times" • Gabriella: "53 groups: put 16 in each"	• What do the horizontal lines represent in Victoria's figure? What do the groupings of vertical lines represent?
Activity 2: Teacher launches the lesson	• Conceptualizing multiplication and representing it in different ways	• Decide on materials to use • Represent (model) multiplication • Communicate work	• Teacher uses two representations of 3 × 11: rods and grid • Teacher compares the rod representation to Victoria's grid	• None significant	• None

Activity 3: Students work in small groups to represent 53 × 16	• Meaning of multiplication	• Model with mathematics
		  → Repeated addition
		  → Area
		  → Base-10 blocks
		• Use tools strategically
		• Reason quantitatively
		• Look for/use structure
		• Attend to precision
		• Look for regularity
		• Communicate thinking
			• 53 blocks and an additional 16 blocks (first group)
			• 8 groups of (100 + 6) (Michael's group)
			• Standard algorithm
			• Numeric representation of partial products (50 + 3) × (10 + 6) (Oscar's group)
			• Repeated addition (Oscar's group)
				• Oscar's group understands multiplication in several different ways. They use several different representations of multiplication (standard algorithm, numeric, partial products, repeated addition) and seem to see the connections among them [37:49]	• One girl in first group counts base-10 rods by 5s and uses 10 to represent 50. Is her number sense poor? Is she having difficulty holding the idea of 5 groups of 10 in her mind?
					• First group of girls counts out 53 blocks and then another 16 [34:56]. Did they get confused by the large numbers, or is their sense of multiplicative relationships weak? How did they get 128 for an answer?

(Continued)

TABLE 6.2 Completed Sample Worksheet: *Multiplication Lesson (Continued)*

Activity Description	Key Mathematical Idea(s)	Mathematical Practices/Habits of Mind	Mathematical Representations	Student Thinking	Errors/Incomplete Thinking; Questions re Thinking
			• 16 rows of 53 (Priscilla's group; the description of this representation didn't match the representation on the poster)	• Michael's group is computationally flexible: —They use doubling to create easier calculations. [39:27] —They understand that they have to compensate for doubling the number of elements in a group by halving the number of groups. —They can use the standard algorithm to multiply using 8 (a single digit) instead of the potentially more error-prone multidigit version (see "error" column for example).	• A couple of groups have trouble calculating 50 × 10, suggesting that they're still developing ideas about place value and multiplication. • One group's answer is 53,318. What did they do and how are they thinking? [43:34] • Small group [49:08] got 128 by applying the standard algorithm incorrectly (they didn't "add a 0" when recording 50 × 16, effectively treating it as 5 × 16). Was this a conceptual or a procedural error?
Activity 4: Students share solutions in whole group	• Meaning of multiplication	• Construct arguments/ critique those of others • Communicate and defend thinking	• Repeated addition • Area model • Base-10 block representation—grid with cut-out squares on top	• Oscar's group: wrote "53" 16 times, separating the digits spatially into one column of 5s and one column of 3s; combined pairs of 53s to get 106, and added the 106s for the answer. [1:03:31]	• Oscar's group's answer is incorrect but seems conceptually sound— some errors seem to be "careless" (e.g., incorrect number of groups, incorrect written answer). Yet it's also not clear that

(Continued)

TABLE 6.2 Completed Sample Worksheet: *Multiplication Lesson (Continued)*

Activity Description	Key Mathematical Idea(s)	Mathematical Practices/Habits of Mind	Mathematical Representations	Student Thinking	Errors/Incomplete Thinking; Questions re Thinking
				• Rodrigo's group used estimation [1:08:46] • Michael's group [1:03:31] added pairs of 53 to get 106, then multiplied 106 × 8 (recognizing that they had half as many groups, but each group had twice as many elements)	Oscar's number sense is developed enough to help him assess the reasonableness of his answers [1:01:58-1:02:00] • Priscilla describes her group's approach: "we put 16 in the rows, and we put 53 columns" [1:07:05], but this doesn't seem to be what they wrote on their poster. Where is the disconnect between verbal description and the representation in the poster? In their thinking? In the physical process of making their poster? • Priscilla's group's answer is 68. How did they arrive at this? Did they (incorrectly) *add* 53 + 16? How does their answer connect to their row/column representation?? What do and don't they understand about multiplication?

* Use evidence from the lesson graph and selective video viewings to back up your analysis

129

130

Section 3

**Putting It
All Together
in the
Classroom**

Commentary on the *Multiplication* Lesson. Like the *Building Triangles* lesson, the *Multiplication* lesson has elements of each of the five lenses we've highlighted. The following aspects of the lesson were salient to us as we considered these five lenses.

The multiplication lesson made substantial cognitive demands on the students in terms of engaging both *conceptual understanding* and *mathematical practices*. Mr. Martinez's focus throughout the lesson was much more on the meaning of multiplication than the accuracy of students' calculations. As students worked to construct two different representations for the situation 16×53, they were challenged to create models, choose and use tools to help them with their work (including using the structure of the number system to help ease their computational burden), and reason quantitatively and attend to precision. (These last practices were variously successful in the different groups and may have been tied to students' ability to use number sense to judge the reasonableness of their work.)

A major focus of this lesson was on ways to *represent* the structure of multiplication. Students identified a variety of ways to model their problem—base-10 blocks, diagrams, repeated addition, expanded notation ($[50 + 3] \times [10 + 6]$), and the "standard" multiplication algorithm. Most (but not all) groups of students created representations and models that reflected the "groups of groups" structure of multiplication. The first group of four girls in the video modeled the problem by counting out 53 blocks (5 rods and 3 unit cubes) and then an additional 16 (1 rod and 6 unit cubes), failing to capture the multiplicative relationship. We wonder about why the girl miscounted the 10 rods. Was it because she simply wasn't paying attention to the problem she was supposed to represent, because she didn't know how to use the manipulatives, or perhaps because she lacked some important conceptual understanding of how you count by groups? Recall that she counted out 10 rods and then skip counted by 5 to find the total number of blocks. She didn't seem troubled by her total (50 instead of 100) and didn't seem to recognize her error even after her group-mate corrected her work by taking 5 of the rods away. In fact, when working on the next problem, she counted by ones on the 10 rods, suggesting that she might not yet know the value of the rod (although she can figure it out).

The lesson offers interesting glimpses into *strengths* as well as *weaknesses* in students' thinking. For example, the students in Michael's group all seemed to understand that they could make "friendlier" numbers and ease their computational burden by doubling 53 to get 106 and then halving the number of groups. Did their choice to work with the base-10 blocks "push" them toward this observation, or did they simply find the blocks a good way to represent knowledge they already had?

Overall, students in the class seemed to be connecting their conceptual understanding of multiplication (as groups of groups) with number sense (what is a reasonable magnitude of the product) and with computational strategies for arriving at the product.

Rodrigo's group actually took on the "reasonable estimate" question, although it's not clear from the video record that they understood how rounding down (to 50) and rounding up (to 20) might affect the actual answer.

Several groups had incorrect answers on their posters; these seemed to reflect different kinds of errors. Oscar's group, for example, seems to have made a "careless" error by failing to check the number of 53s they added (13 instead of 16) and then further compounding the error by writing the answer to the computation 53 × 13 as 589 instead of 689, even though Oscar mentally made the correct calculations. (The video records him mentally adding 3 to 36 to get 39, recording the 3—which he calls "30"— at the top of the column of 5s and writing down the "9" under the horizontal line that separates the columns from the answer. He then counts thirteen 5s. Instead of computing 5 × 13 directly he multiplies 5 × 10 to get 50, then says "5 times 12 is 60, 65" and then adds in the 3 he'd recorded, saying "68." Somehow, however, the answer is recorded as 589 instead of 689 [~52:33−52:57].) While the boys may not have stopped to ask themselves whether their 589 was a reasonable answer they did seem to understand that they could represent the structure of multiplication in several different ways. Furthermore, while their mental addition of thirteen 53s (aided by their knowledge of multiplication facts) was off by 100, they did at least have the correct order of magnitude.

Several students seemed to be working on the idea of multiplying by 10. In a couple of groups, students struggled over the product of 50 × 10 and seemed to resort to the "add a zero" rule rather than understanding that the product can be thought of as 10 groups of 50 (a problem that is easily solved by skip counting, for example). The group that got 128 using the standard algorithm, solving it as

$$
\begin{array}{r}
{}^{1}16 \\
\times\ 53 \\
\hline
48 \\
+80 \\
\hline
128
\end{array}
\qquad \text{instead of} \qquad
\begin{array}{r}
{}^{1}16 \\
\times\ 53 \\
\hline
48 \\
+800 \\
\hline
848
\end{array}
$$

may either have made a "careless" error or may not have understood that the digit 5 in the number 53 really represents five groups of 10 and therefore that, when multiplying the 6 in 16 by the 5 they were really multiplying 6 by 50. (If the group had made a careless error, the lack of care extended to their acceptance of the product as well, since 128 isn't a reasonable answer—given that *two* 53s is nearly 128, sixteen 53s would be substantially larger than 128.)

Other students' errors clearly point to the need for more conceptual development. Priscilla's group's answer of 68 suggests that they may have added 53 and 16 (albeit incorrectly). If this interpretation of their work is correct, we could surmise that students in this group had yet to internalize the central idea that multiplication doesn't operate on individual numbers but on groups of numbers. We haven't been able to

132

Section 3

**Putting It
All Together
in the
Classroom**

develop a plausible explanation for the group that answered 53,318; surely more information about their reasoning would be called for.

Mr. Martinez's responses to the students' presentations, as well as his wrap-up demonstration using a grid model to identify "subparts" of the problem that are amenable to easier computation, suggest that his focus for the lesson was on having students understand how to think multiplicatively and not on correct computation. He didn't dismiss incorrect answers as irrelevant but seemed to treat errors in the context of sense making—focusing on whether answers were reasonable—and as something that could be addressed with more attention or work. His focus on sense making can also be seen in his use of Rodrigo's group's work to highlight the value of estimating the magnitude of a reasonable answer.

Some Additional Points of Reflection. As you did with the *Building Triangles* exercise, take a few more minutes to reflect on what it was like to review the lesson graph and view this video while keeping several perspectives going simultaneously.

- Were both of the artifacts—lesson graph and video—useful to you? How did you use them?

- Were you able to analyze and provide evidence for all five perspectives represented by the columns in the worksheet?

- Did some of the perspectives feel more useful than others in terms of thinking about students' learning?

- How was what you noticed similar and different from what your colleagues (or we) noticed? Did you find things that we didn't take note of?

Linking to Your Own Practice

The two exercises in this chapter have focused on integrating the various lenses we've ground and polished in earlier chapters. Our goal has been to support you in identifying and investigating each of the lenses as they emerge and interact over the course of a classroom lesson. We hope that, by practicing with them here, you'll become better able to focus on them in your own teaching as well. We also hope that this more integrated approach will help to provide you with increased awareness of the importance of the following:

- Examining the important mathematical content and practices in the tasks you pose for your students (tasks that may be part of your curriculum materials or that you find or develop on your own)

- Planning for and using mathematical representations to support and promote student understanding

- Recognizing and capitalizing on the potential logic in students' thinking, including the logic in their errors and/or misunderstandings

- Identifying common errors and/or misunderstandings and explicitly planning to use them for instructional purposes

As we close this book, we encourage you to think about how you gather evidence to guide your own instructional decision making. For example, how do you decide whether a lesson, overall, was successful? What kinds of evidence do you collect to inform you about what (and how) your students understand the mathematics they are working on?

Some of the information you gather is probably formative in that you're collecting it in real time as you move through a lesson and you're using it to make instructional decisions to keep the lesson moving smoothly and productively. There are many ways to gather information on the fly, for example, observing students as they work, asking students to report on their own understanding of a particular idea or problem with a thumbs up or a thumbs down, collecting quick responses to problems or questions on whiteboards or with a show of hands, and asking students questions to clarify their thinking for you or to push on their ideas.

On occasion, it's also useful to take the time to engage in more in-depth analysis of an entire lesson. Consider videotaping one of your classes and constructing a lesson graph yourself (we've provided you with a template in the Appendix and as a writeable PDF on PDToolKit). It's an interesting exercise to try because it gives you the chance to step back and see how the class unfolded from more of an outside perspective rather than relying only on your memory of how the lesson felt while you were in the thick of it. Analyze your own lesson graph as we did here by filling out a Chapter 6 worksheet and consulting with the video, if needed, at points that you feel are particularly noteworthy. As you explore your lesson, focus on some of the following:

- Articulate the goals of your lesson in terms of key mathematical ideas and practices (the first column of the Chapter 6 worksheet).

- Review the lesson graph and see how the lesson as it actually played out mapped onto your goals.

- Look for evidence of students' thinking in terms of both mathematical strengths and weaknesses.

- Consider how students' thinking developed over the course of the lesson.

- Think about how the representations you used in class supported students' thinking and/or illuminated different aspects of the mathematics under study.

- Look for evidence of students' errors or underdeveloped thinking.

- Think about how your "during class" impressions of students' work and ideas squared with your post-lesson analysis of the video.

- Some teachers overestimate how many (and which) of their students were really with them in class—did you?

Final Thoughts

As a teacher, you are called on to make hundreds of decisions over the course of a day in a fast-paced, moment-to-moment environment. Where you focus your attention and how you interpret what you see and hear are key to how you make those decisions. We believe that classroom artifacts such as student work, video of classroom interactions, curriculum tasks and lesson plans, and lesson graphs can be powerful vehicles for improving practice by removing aspects of the classroom learning and teaching from the immediacy of the classroom itself and examining them in settings that allow more careful, considered analysis.

We hope that the artifacts we've used in this book have given you the opportunity to explore various classroom events and student work without the real-time pressure of having to register, interpret, and respond to such events as they unfold within your own classrooms. In addition, we hope that this book has provided you an opportunity to develop and practice new ways to listen to students, interpret their thinking, and plan lessons that are responsive to the particular strengths and needs of the students in *your* class. We wrote this book to support you in using classroom artifacts to hone in on student thinking and errors, mathematical content and practices, and mathematical representations. We all improve our understanding of teaching and learning mathematics through the interplay of study and practice, and we hope that you and your colleagues will continue to turn to evidence from artifacts to inform your teaching.

Appendix

PDToolkit

for

Examining Mathematics Practice through Classroom Artifacts

See PDToolkit online to download writable PDF worksheets.

*Writable PDF Worksheet

Key Mathematical Ideas:

My Descriptions	My Interpretations and Supporting Evidence	Alternative Interpretations?	My Questions

Name: Francesca

Carolyn's mom brought 8 brownies to Carolyn's dance group. That day 6 girls were there. If they share the brownies equally, how much does each girl get?

6 R 2

each girl gets 1 brownie

Name: Sahgar

Carolyn's mom brought 8 brownies to Carolyn's dance group. That day 6 girls were there. If they share the brownies equally, how much does each girl get? 1 and 3 brownies

$$\begin{array}{r} 3 \\ 30\overline{)100} \\ -90 \\ \hline 10 \end{array}$$

13

$$\begin{array}{r} 6\;\;8 \\ -6 \\ \hline 2 \end{array}$$

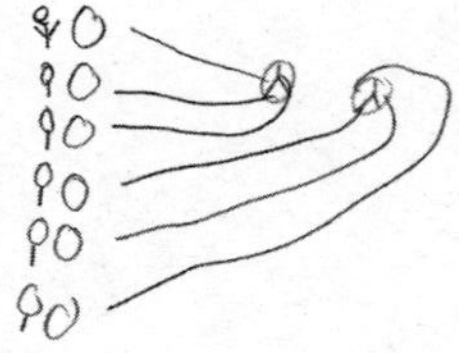

30/5
30.5
32
47.5

Name: _____

Carolyn's mom brought 8 brownies to Carolyn's dance group. That day 6 girls were there. If they share the brownies equally, how much does each girl get?

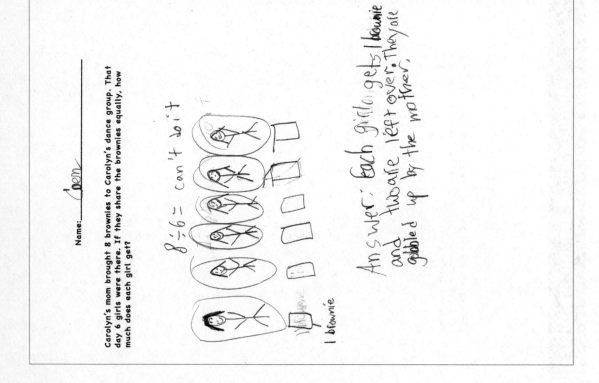

$8 \div 6 =$ can't do it

1 brownie

Answer: Each girl gets 1 brownie and two are left over. They are gobbled up by the mother.

Name: Andice

Carolyn's mom brought 8 brownies to Carolyn's dance group. That day 6 girls were there. If they share the brownies equally, how much does each girl get?

8 cookies

$\frac{6}{8}$ taken

$1\frac{1}{6}$ per child

2 left
split
turn to thirds per cookie

Name: Annie

Carolyn's mom brought 8 brownies to Carolyn's dance group. That day 6 girls were there. If they share the brownies equally, how much does each girl get?

$8 \div 6 = 1.4$ Answer = 1.4

⊗ = Brownie

♀ = girls

taly marks = 8 pieces of Brownie

Name: Lauren M.

Carolyn's mom brought 8 brownies to Carolyn's dance group. That day 6 girls were there. If they share the brownies equally, how much does each girl get?

8 brownies
6 girls

each girl gets 1 cookie and there is one left over.

Name: Ollie R.

Carolyn's mom brought 8 brownies to Carolyn's dance group. That day 6 girls were there. If they share the brownies equally, how much does each girl get?

$8 \div 6 = 1R2$

$6 + 2 = 8$

$2 = R2$

$8 \div 8 = 1$

$R2 + 1 = 1R2$ brownies

Name: Joe

Carolyn's mom brought 8 brownies to Carolyn's dance group. That day 6 girls were there. If they share the brownies equally, how much does each girl get?

$\dfrac{2}{6} = \dfrac{1}{3}$

$$\begin{array}{r} 1\frac{2}{6} \\ 6\overline{)8} \\ -6 \\ \hline 2 \end{array}$$

$\left(1\frac{1}{3}\text{ brownies for each girl}\right)$

$1\frac{1}{3} \times 6 = 8$

$1\frac{1}{3} \times 3 = 4$

$4 \times 2 = 8$

140

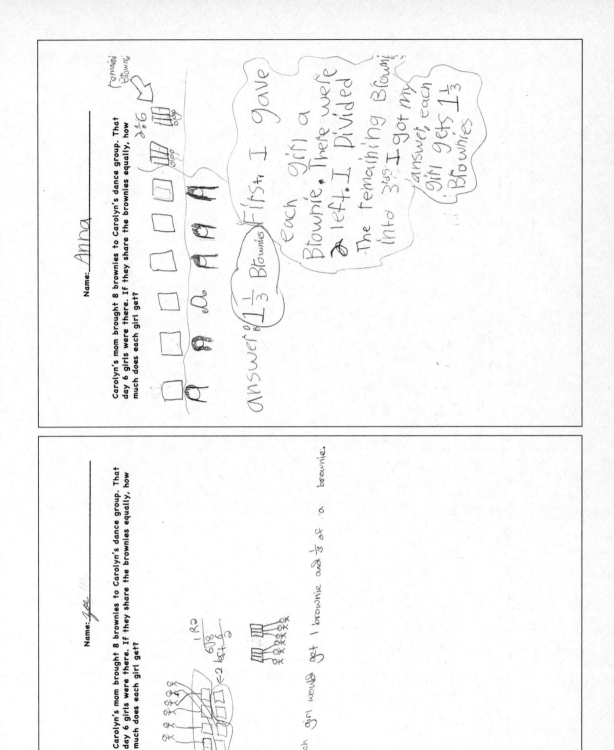

Name: Anna

Carolyn's mom brought 8 brownies to Carolyn's dance group. That day 6 girls were there. If they share the brownies equally, how much does each girl get?

remaining Brownie

Answer: $1\frac{1}{3}$ Brownies

First, I gave each girl a Brownie. There were 2 left. I Divided The remaining Brownies into 3rds. I got my answer, each girl gets $1\frac{1}{3}$ Brownies

---

Name: Joe

Carolyn's mom brought 8 brownies to Carolyn's dance group. That day 6 girls were there. If they share the brownies equally, how much does each girl get?

Each girl would get 1 brownie and $\frac{1}{3}$ of a brownie.

141

Name: Aidan

Carolyn's mom brought 8 brownies to Carolyn's dance group. That day 6 girls were there. If they share the brownies equally, how much does each girl get?

I think they split the 2 extra brownies into 3rds so 2×3 = 6 and that howmany girls their are so the answer is (6.3)

Name: Cyruss G

Carolyn's mom brought 8 brownies to Carolyn's dance group. That day 6 girls were there. If they share the brownies equally, how much does each girl get?

6 girls

8 brownies

If you give 1 brownie to each girl and if you give 2 left over each girl, that it would go over. 2 brownies would go over. I divid it into sixths, that would give each girl 1 2/6 or 1 1/3.

Carolyn's mom brought 8 brownies to Carolyn's dance group. That day 6 girls were there. If they share the brownies equally, how much does each girl get?

▢ ▢ ▢ ▢ ▢ ▢ ▢ ▢ 8 brownies

they each get 1 ∩ 4/7

Carolyn's mom brought 8 brownies to Carolyn's dance group. That day 6 girls were there. If they share the brownies equally, how much does each girl get?

1 12 brownies   1 to
8/8
6/2

I first did 8 go into 6 how many times does
over so then I divided each into
three parts so then 3×2= 6 parts so
each kid gets 1 and 1/3

with's once with 2 left

143

Chapter 3 Worksheet: Examining Errors and Misconceptions

Key Mathematical Ideas:

Error or Misconception	Potential (what the student knows)	New Insights and/or Curiosities

Chapter 4 Worksheet 1: Examining Your Textbook

Unit Title:

	Thoughts/Comments:
What key concepts (big ideas) does the unit focus on?	
What key knowledge and skills does the unit emphasize?	Thoughts/Comments:

Chapter Title:

	Thoughts/Comments:
What key concepts (big ideas) does this chapter focus on?	
How does the work in this chapter engage mathematical practices/habits of mind?	Thoughts/Comments:
What key knowledge and skills does this chapter emphasize?	Thoughts/Comments:
What are the explicit connections to other chapters in the unit?	Thoughts/Comments:

Chapter 4 Worksheet 2: Analyzing a Lesson

Lesson:

Task	Math Skills Emphasized?	Math Concepts Emphasized?	Math Practices/Habits of Mind Emphasized?	Task Demands
Activity 1:				
Activity 2:				
Activity 3:				
Activity 4:				

Chapter 5 Worksheet: Connecting Representations

Mathematical Task (note the task and key mathematical ideas)	Representations/Approaches	Analysis and Connection of Representations

Chapter 6 Worksheet: Integrated Analysis of a Lesson

Lesson:

Use evidence from the lesson graph and selective video viewings to back up your analysis.

Activity Description	Key Mathematical Idea(s)	Key Mathematical Practices/Habits of Mind	Key Mathematical Representations	Student Thinking	Errors/Incomplete Thinking; Questions re: Thinking
Activity 1:					
Activity 2:					
Activity 3:					
Activity 4:					

[45–minute lesson]   **Building Triangles: A Sixth-Grade Lesson**

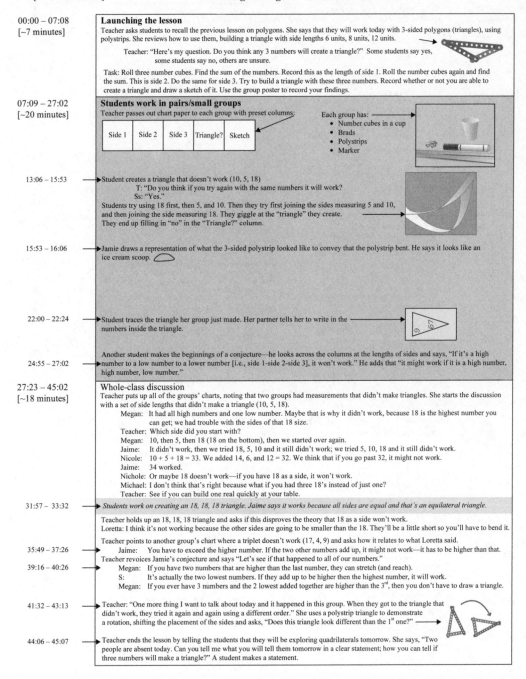

00:00 – 07:08
[~7 minutes]

Launching the lesson

Teacher asks students to recall the previous lesson on polygons. She says that they will work today with 3-sided polygons (triangles), using polystrips. She reviews how to use them, building a triangle with side lengths 6 units, 8 units, 12 units.

Teacher: "Here's my question. Do you think any 3 numbers will create a triangle?" Some students say yes, some students say no, others are unsure.

Task: Roll three number cubes. Find the sum of the numbers. Record this as the length of side 1. Roll the number cubes again and find the sum. This is side 2. Do the same for side 3. Try to build a triangle with these three numbers. Record whether or not you are able to create a triangle and draw a sketch of it. Use the group poster to record your findings.

07:09 – 27:02
[~20 minutes]

Students work in pairs/small groups

Teacher passes out chart paper to each group with preset columns:

Side 1	Side 2	Side 3	Triangle?	Sketch

Each group has:
- Number cubes in a cup
- Brads
- Polystrips
- Marker

13:06 – 15:53

Student creates a triangle that doesn't work (10, 5, 18).
 T: "Do you think if you try again with the same numbers it will work?"
 Ss: "Yes."
Students try using 18 first, then 5, and 10. Then they try first joining the sides measuring 5 and 10, and then joining the side measuring 18. They giggle at the "triangle" they create.
They end up filling in "no" in the "Triangle?" column.

15:53 – 16:06

Jamie draws a representation of what the 3-sided polystrip looked like to convey that the polystrip bent. He says it looks like an ice cream scoop.

22:00 – 22:24

Student traces the triangle her group just made. Her partner tells her to write in the numbers inside the triangle.

24:55 – 27:02

Another student makes the beginnings of a conjecture—he looks across the columns at the lengths of sides and says, "If it's a high number to a low number [i.e., side 1-side 2-side 3], it won't work." He adds that "it might work if it is a high number, high number, low number."

27:23 – 45:02
[~18 minutes]

Whole-class discussion

Teacher puts up all of the groups' charts, noting that two groups had measurements that didn't make triangles. She starts the discussion with a set of side lengths that didn't make a triangle (10, 5, 18).

 Megan: It had all high numbers and one low number. Maybe that is why it didn't work, because 18 is the highest number you can get; we had trouble with the sides of that 18 size.
 Teacher: Which side did you start with?
 Megan: 10, then 5, then 18 (18 on the bottom), then we started over again.
 Jaime: It didn't work, then we tried 18, 5, 10 and it still didn't work; we tried 5, 10, 18 and it still didn't work.
 Nicole: 10 + 5 + 18 = 33. We added 14, 6, and 12 = 32. We think that if you go past 32, it might not work.
 Jaime: 34 worked.
 Nichole: Or maybe 18 doesn't work—if you have 18 as a side, it won't work.
 Michael: I don't think that's right because what if you had three 18's instead of just one?
 Teacher: See if you can build one real quickly at your table.

31:57 – 33:32

Students work on creating an 18, 18, 18 triangle. Jaime says it works because all sides are equal and that's an equilateral triangle.

Teacher holds up an 18, 18, 18 triangle and asks if this disproves the theory that 18 as a side won't work.
Loretta: I think it's not working because the other sides are going to be smaller than the 18. They'll be a little short so you'll have to bend it.

Teacher points to another group's chart where a triplet doesn't work (17, 4, 9) and asks how it relates to what Loretta said.

35:49 – 37:26

 Jaime: You have to exceed the higher number. If the two other numbers add up, it might not work—it has to be higher than that.
Teacher revoices Jamie's conjecture and says "Let's see if that happened to all of our numbers."

39:16 – 40:26

 Megan: If you have two numbers that are higher than the last number, they can stretch (and reach).
 S: It's actually the two lowest numbers. If they add up to be higher than the highest number, it will work.
 Megan: If you ever have 3 numbers and the 2 lowest added together are higher than the 3rd, then you don't have to draw a triangle.

41:32 – 43:13

Teacher: "One more thing I want to talk about today and it happened in this group. When they got to the triangle that didn't work, they tried it again and again using a different order." She uses a polystrip triangle to demonstrate a rotation, shifting the placement of the sides and asks, "Does this triangle look different than the 1st one?"

44:06 – 45:07

Teacher ends the lesson by telling the students that they will be exploring quadrilaterals tomorrow. She says, "Two people are absent today. Can you tell me what you will tell them tomorrow in a clear statement; how you can tell if three numbers will make a triangle?" A student makes a statement.

Multiplication: A Fourth-Grade Lesson

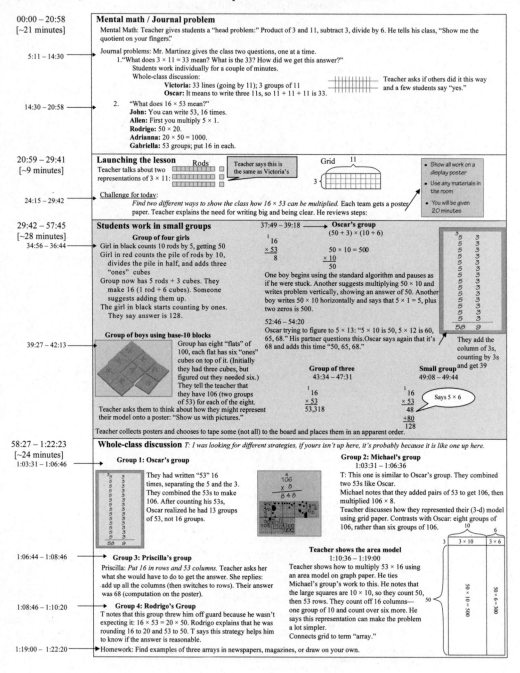

00:00 – 20:58 [~21 minutes]	**Mental math / Journal problem** Mental Math: Teacher gives students a "head problem:" Product of 3 and 11, subtract 3, divide by 6. He tells his class, "Show me the quotient on your fingers."

5:11 – 14:30	Journal problems: Mr. Martinez gives the class two questions, one at a time.
	  1."What does 3 × 11 = 33 mean? What is the 33? How did we get this answer?"
	    Students work individually for a couple of minutes.
	    Whole-class discussion:
	      Victoria: 33 lines (going by 11); 3 groups of 11 Teacher asks if others did it this way
	      Oscar: It means to write three 11s, so 11 + 11 + 11 is 33. and a few students say "yes."

14:30 – 20:58	2. "What does 16 × 53 mean?"
	    John: You can write 53, 16 times.
	    Allen: First you multiply 5 × 1.
	    Rodrigo: 50 × 20.
	    Adrianna: 20 × 50 = 1000.
	    Gabriella: 53 groups; put 16 in each.

20:59 – 29:41
[~9 minutes]

Launching the lesson   Rods   Teacher says this is   Grid   11
Teacher talks about two   the same as Victoria's
representations of 3 × 11:

- Show all work on a display poster
- Use any materials in the room
- You will be given 20 minutes

24:15 – 29:42

Challenge for today:
    Find two different ways to show the class how 16 × 53 can be multiplied. Each team gets a poster
    paper. Teacher explains the need for writing big and being clear. He reviews steps:

29:42 – 57:45
[~28 minutes]
34:56 – 36:44

Students work in small groups   37:49 – 39:18 → **Oscar's group**
    Group of four girls   (50 + 3) × (10 + 6)
Girl in black counts 10 rods by 5, getting 50
Girl in red counts the pile of rods by 10,
    divides the pile in half, and adds three
    "ones" cubes
Group now has 5 rods + 3 cubes. They
    make 16 (1 rod + 6 cubes). Someone
    suggests adding them up.
The girl in black starts counting by ones.
    They say answer is 128.

$$\begin{array}{r} 16 \\ \times\ 53 \\ \hline 8 \end{array}$$
50 × 10 = 500
$$\begin{array}{r} \times\ 10 \\ \hline 50 \end{array}$$

One boy begins using the standard algorithm and pauses as
if he were stuck. Another suggests multiplying 50 × 10 and
writes problem vertically, showing an answer of 50. Another
boy writes 50 × 10 horizontally and says that 5 × 1 = 5, plus
two zeros is 500.

52:46 – 54:20
Oscar trying to figure to 5 × 13: "5 × 10 is 50, 5 × 12 is 60,
65, 68." His partner questions this. Oscar says again that it's
68 and adds this time "50, 65, 68."

They add the
column of 3s,
counting by 3s
and get 39

39:27 – 42:13

Group of boys using base-10 blocks
Group has eight "flats" of
100, each flat has six "ones"
cubes on top of it. (Initially
they had three cubes, but
figured out they needed six.)
They tell the teacher that
they have 106 (two groups
of 53) for each of the eight.
Teacher asks them to think about how they might represent
their model onto a poster: "Show us with pictures."

Group of three
43:34 – 47:31
$$\begin{array}{r} 16 \\ \times\ 53 \\ \hline 53,318 \end{array}$$

Small group
49:08 – 49:44
$$\begin{array}{r} 16 \\ \times\ 53 \\ \hline 48 \\ +80 \\ \hline 128 \end{array}$$
Says 5 × 6

Teacher collects posters and chooses to tape some (not all) to the board and places them in an apparent order.

58:27 – 1:22:23
[~24 minutes]
1:03:31 – 1:06:46

Whole-class discussion *T: I was looking for different strategies, if yours isn't up here, it's probably because it is like one up here.*

Group 1: Oscar's group

They had written "53" 16
times, separating the 5 and the 3.
They combined the 53s to make
106. After counting his 53s,
Oscar realized he had 13 groups
of 53, not 16 groups.

Group 2: Michael's group
1:03:31 – 1:06:36
T: This one is similar to Oscar's group. They combined
two 53s like Oscar.
Michael notes that they added pairs of 53 to get 106, then
multiplied 106 × 8.
Teacher discusses how they represented their (3-d) model
using grid paper. Contrasts with Oscar: eight groups of
106, rather than six groups of 106.

$$\begin{array}{r} 106 \\ \times\ 8 \\ \hline 848 \end{array}$$

1:06:44 – 1:08:46

Group 3: Priscilla's group
Priscilla: *Put 16 in rows and 53 columns.* Teacher asks her
what she would have to do to get the answer. She replies:
add up all the columns (then switches to rows). Their answer
was 68 (computation on the poster).

Teacher shows the area model
1:10:36 – 1:19:00
Teacher shows how to multiply 53 × 16 using
an area model on graph paper. He ties
Michael's group's work to this. He notes that
the large squares are 10 × 10, so they count 50,
then 53 rows. They count off 16 columns—
one group of 10 and count over six more. He
says this representation can make the problem
a lot simpler.
Connects grid to term "array."

1:08:46 – 1:10:20

Group 4: Rodrigo's Group
T notes that this group threw him off guard because he wasn't
expecting it: 16 × 53 = 20 × 50. Rodrigo explains that he was
rounding 16 to 20 and 53 to 50. T says this strategy helps him
to know if the answer is reasonable.

	10	6
3	3 × 10	3 × 6
50	50 × 10 = 500	50 × 6 = 300

1:19:00 – 1:22:20

Homework: Find examples of three arrays in newspapers, magazines, or draw on your own.

[____ minute
lesson]

Lesson _____ **Grade Level** _____

[____ minutes] | **First activity:**

[____ minutes] | **Second activity:**

[____ minutes] | **Third activity:**

Hints: If you are completing the lesson graph electronically, text boxes may offer you more flexibility in placing text. For activities in which students work independently, shade rows gray. Make sure the heights of each row is proportionate to the amount of time spent on the activity during class. If the lesson has four activities or more, insert row(s) as needed.

References

Allen, D., & Blythe, T. (2004). *The facilitators' book of questions: Tools for looking together at teacher and student work.* New York: Teachers College Press.

Ball, D. L. (1992, Summer). Magical hopes: Manipulatives and the reform of math education. *American Educator, 16*(2), 14–18, 46–47.

Ball, D. L., & Bass, H. (2000). Interweaving content and pedagogy in teaching and learning to teach: Knowing and using mathematics. In J. Boaler (Ed.), *Multiple perspectives on the teaching and learning of mathematics* (pp. 83–104). Westport, CT: Ablex.

Ball, D. L., Thames, M. H., & Phelps, G. (2008). Content knowledge for teaching: What makes it special? *Journal of Teacher Education, 59*(5), 389–407.

Black, P., Harrison, C., Lee, C., Marshall, B., & Wiliam, D. (2003). *Assessment for learning: Putting it into practice.* New York: Open University Press.

Black, P., & Wiliam, D. (1998). Inside the black box: Raising standards through classroom assessment. *Phi Delta Kappan, 80*, 139–148.

Blythe, T., Allen, D., & Powell, B. S. (1999). *Looking together at student work: A companion guide to assessing student learning.* New York: Teachers College Press.

Borasi, R. (1987). Exploring mathematics through the analysis of errors. *For the Learning of Mathematics, 7*(3), 2–8.

Borasi, R. (1996). *Reconceiving mathematics instruction: A focus on errors.* Norwood, NJ: Ablex.

Borko, H., Jacobs, J., Eiteljorg, E., & Pittman, M. E. (2008). Video as a tool for fostering productive discussions in mathematics professional development. *Teaching and Teacher Education, 24,* 417–436.

Burns, M. (2010, February). Snapshots of student misunderstanding. *Educational Leadership, 67*(5), 18–22.

Buswell, G. T., & Lenore, J. (1926). *Diagnostic studies in arithmetic.* Supplementary Educational Monographs 30. Chicago: University of Chicago Press.

Carpenter, T. P., Franke, M. L., & Levi, L. (2003). *Thinking mathematically: Integrating arithmetic and algebra in elementary school.* Portsmouth, NH: Heinemann.

Chabris, C., & Simons, D. (2010). *The invisible gorilla and other ways our intuitions deceive us.* New York: Crown.

Common Core State Standards. (2010). http://www.corestandards.org.

Cunningham, P. M., & Cunningham J. W. (2010). *What really matters in writing: Research-based practices across the curriculum.* Boston: Pearson.

Cuoco, A., Goldenberg, E. P., & Mark, J. (1996). Habits of mind: An organizing principle for mathematics curriculum. *Journal of Mathematical Behavior, 15*(4), 375–402.

Cuoco, A., Goldenberg, E. P., & Mark, J. (2010). Organizing a curriculum around mathematical habits of mind. *Mathematics Teacher, 103*(9), 682–689.

Driscoll, M. (1999). *Fostering algebraic thinking.* Portsmouth, NH: Heinemann

Driscoll, M. (2007). *Fostering geometric thinking.* Portsmouth, NH: Heinemann.

Fosnot, C. T., & Dolk, M. (2001). *Young mathematicians at work.* Portsmouth, NH: Heinemann.

Goldsmith, L. T., & Seago, N. (2011). Using classroom artifacts to focus teachers' noticing: Affordances and opportunities. In M. G. Sherin, V. R. Jacobs, & R. A. Philipp (Eds.), *Mathematics teacher noticing: Seeing through teachers' eyes* (pp. 169–187). London: Routledge.

Henningsen, M., & Stein, M. K. (1997). Mathematical tasks and student cognition: Classroom-based factors that support and inhibit high-level mathematical thinking and reasoning. *Journal for Research in Mathematics Education, 28*(5), 524–549.

Heritage, M. (2010). *Formative assessment: Making it happen in the classroom.* Thousand Oaks, CA: Corwin.

Hiebert, J., Gallimore, R., Garnier, H., Givvin, K. B., Hollingsworth, H., Jacobs, J., Chui, A. M., Wearne, D., Smith, M., Kersting, N., Manaster, A., Tseng, E., Etterbeek, W., Manaster, C., Gonzales, P., & Stigler, J. (2003). *Highlights from the TIMSS 1999 Video Study of Eighth Grade Mathematics Teaching,* NCES (2003–011), U.S. Department of Education. Washington, DC: National Center for Education Statistics.

Jacobs, V. R., Lamb, L. L. C., & Philipp, R. A. (2010). Professional noticing of children's mathematical thinking. *Journal for Research in Mathematics Education, 41*(2), 169–202.

Jones, C. F. (1991). *Mistakes that worked.* New York: Delacorte Press.

Lappan, G., Fey, J. T., Fitzgerald, W. M., Friel, S. N., & Phillips, E. D. (1998). *Connected mathematics. Shapes and designs: Two-dimensional geometry. Teachers' guide.* Menlo Park, CA: Dale Seymour Publications.

Lave, J. (1988). *Cognition in practice: Mind, mathematics, and culture in everyday life.* Cambridge: Cambridge University Press.

Lave, J., & Wenger, E. (1991). *Situated learning: Legitimate peripheral participation.* Cambridge: Cambridge University Press.

Mason, J. (2002). *Researching your own practice: The discipline of noticing.* London: Routledge Falmer.

National Council of Teachers of Mathematics. (1989). *Curriculum and evaluation standards for school mathematics.* Reston, VA: Author.

National Council of Teachers of Mathematics. (1991). *Principles and standards for school mathematics.* Reston, VA: Author.

National Council of Teachers of Mathematics. (2000). *Professional standards for teaching mathematics.* Reston, VA: Author.

National Council of Teachers of Mathematics. (2006). *Curriculum focal points for prekindergarten through grade 8 mathematics.* Reston, VA: Author.

Nikula, J., Goldsmith, L. T., Blasi, Z. V., & Seago, N. (2006). A framework for the strategic use of classroom artifacts in mathematics professional development. *National Council of Supervisors of Mathematics Journal of Mathematics Education Leadership, 9*(1), 57–64.

Piaget, J. (1970). Piaget's theory. In P. H. Mussen (Ed.), *Carmichael's manual of child psychology.* (Vol. 2, pp. 703–732). New York: Wiley.

Piaget, J., & Szeminska, A. (1952). *The child's conception of number.* London: Routledge & Kegan Paul.

Resnick, L. B., & Zurawsky, C. (Eds.). (2006, March). Do the math: Cognitive demand makes a difference. *AERA Research Points 4*(2), 1–4.

Santagata, R., Zannoni, C., & Stigler, J. W. (2007). The role of lesson analysis in pre-service teacher education: An empirical investigation of teacher learning from a virtual video-based field experience. *Journal of Mathematics Teacher Education, 10*(2), 123–140.

Schifter, D. (Ed.). (1996). *What's happening in math class? Envisioning new practices through teacher narratives.* New York: Teachers College Press.

Schifter, D., Bastable, V., & Russell, S. J. (2010a). *Building a system of tens: Calculating with whole numbers and decimals. Facilitator guide* (2nd ed.). Boston: Pearson.

Schifter, D., Bastable, V., & Russell, S. J. (2010b). *Making meaning of numbers in the domains of whole numbers and fractions. Facilitator guide* (2nd ed.). Boston: Pearson.

Schifter, D., & Fosnot, C. T. (1993). *Reconstructing mathematics education: Stories of teachers meeting the challenge of reform.* New York: Teachers College Press.

Seago, N. (2004). Using video as an object of inquiry for mathematics teaching and learning. In J. Brophy (Ed.), *Advances in research on teaching: Vol. 10. Using video in teacher education* (pp. 259–286). Oxford: Elsevier.

Seago, N., Driscoll, M., Callahan, P., Jacobs, J., Nikula, J. (in press). *Learning and teaching geometry: Videocases for professional development.* San Francisco: WestEd.

Seago, N., & Goldsmith, L. T. (2006). *Learning mathematics for teaching.* In J. Novotna, H. Moraova, M. Kratka, & N. Stehlikova (Eds.), *Proceedings of the 30th Conference of the International Group for the Psychology of Mathematics Education* (Vol. 5, pp. 73–80). Prague: PME.

Seago, N., Mumme, J., & Branca, N. (2004). *Learning and teaching linear functions.* Portsmouth, NH: Heinemann.

Sherin, M. G. (2004). New perspectives on the role of video in teacher education. In J. Brophy (Ed.), *Advances in research on teaching: Vol. 10. Using video in teacher education* (pp. 1–27). New York: Elsevier.

Sherin, M. G., Jacobs, V. R., & Philipp, R. A. (Eds.). (2011). *Mathematics teacher noticing: Seeing through teachers' eyes.* New York: Routledge.

Shulman, L. S. (1986). Those who understand teach: Knowledge growth in teaching. *Educational Researcher, 57*(1), 1–22.

Smith, M. S., & Stein, M. K. (1998). Selecting and creating mathematical tasks: From research to practice. *Teaching Mathematics in the Middle School, 3*(5), 344–350.

Star, J. R., & Strickland, S. K. (2008). Learning to observe: Using video to improve pre-service mathematics teachers' ability to notice. *Journal of Mathematics Teacher Education, 11,* 107–125.

Stein, M. K., Grover, B., & Henningsen, M. (1996). Building student capacity for mathematical thinking and reasoning: An analysis of mathematical tasks used in reform classrooms. *American Educational Research Journal, 33*(2), 455–488.

Stein, M. K., Smith, M. S., Henningsen, M. A., & Silver, E. A. (2009). *Implementing standards-based mathematics instruction: A casebook for professional development* (2nd ed.). New York: Teachers College Press.

van de Walle, J. A. (2004). *Elementary and middle school mathematics: Teaching developmentally* (5th ed.). Boston: Pearson.

van Es, E. A. (2011). A framework for learning to notice. In M. G. Sherin, V. R. Jacobs, & R. A. Philipp, *Mathematics teacher noticing: Seeing through teachers' eyes* (pp. 134–151). London: Routledge.

van Es, E. A., & Sherin, M. G. (2008). Mathematics teachers' "learning to notice" in the context of a video club. *Teaching and Teacher Education, 24*(2), 244–276.

Wearne, D., Murray, H., Hiebert, J., Fuson, K. C., Fennema, E., & Carpenter, T. P. (1997). *Making sense: Teaching and learning mathematics with understanding.* Portsmouth, NH: Heinemann.

Werner, H. (1948). *Comparative psychology of mental development.* New York: International Universities Press, Inc.

Wertsch, J. V. (1985). *Vygotsky and the social formation of mind.* Cambridge, MA: Harvard University Press.

Book Study Guide for Examining Mathematics Practice Through Classroom Artifacts

Book Study Guidelines[1]

Reading, reacting, and interacting with others about a book is one of the ways we process new information. Book studies are a common feature in many school districts because they recognize the power of collaborative learning. The intent of a book study is to provide a supportive context for accessing new ideas and continuing to develop effective instructional practices. Before you begin, you have some decisions to make about how your study group will work: who will facilitate discussions, how you'll structure your sessions, and how you will select questions to guide your discussions.

Deciding on a Facilitator

Before you select a discussion structure, you'll need to figure out how to facilitate your discussions. The facilitator will be responsible for moving the discussion along in order to address the most important issues for the group. If your group decides to keep notes of your meetings, the facilitator may also act as the official note taker, distributing notes to group members after the session is over. Since many school districts require documentation for book studies, the facilitator can also be responsible for filing any necessary documentation with the appropriate administrative person and also providing copies to all group members for their records.

There are basically two ways to organize study group facilitation—either rotate the role session by session among study group members or have a single facilitator take responsibility for all sessions. If you choose the former approach, group members might volunteer for sessions, or you might just draw lots at the end of a

---

[1] Adapted from Cunningham and Cunningham (2010).

session to identify the next session's facilitator. If you take the single-facilitator approach, the facilitator might be someone who read the book first and suggested it to the group or perhaps your district math coordinator or math coach.

Structuring Your Book Study Sessions

Here are several possible structures to choose from in designing your book study sessions.

Structure 1: Using the Reading Reaction Sheet

One way to structure your book discussion of *Examining Mathematics Practice Through Classroom Artifacts* is to use the Reading Reaction Sheet on page 162 and as a writeable PDF on PDToolKit. For each chapter, the facilitator first makes a copy of the Reading Reaction Sheet for each group member. The facilitator begins the session by explaining that the first question on the Reading Reaction Sheet is intended to start the group discussion. The group then generates three additional questions before the whole-group discussion starts.

There are a couple of ways to identify the additional discussion questions. The facilitator can ask each person to propose at least one question and then let the group choose the three they want to discuss. Alternatively, the facilitator can break participants into three groups and have each group be responsible for identifying one question for the discussion. Your study group might identify yet another process for generating the three additional questions.

Once you have settled on your questions, begin your discussion with question 1. The facilitator's job is to make sure that the discussion connects the questions to the chapter's key ideas and to help participants connect these ideas to their own situations.

Structure 2: Chapter Guiding Questions

Another possible structure involves basing the study group discussion on the guiding questions that are provided in this study guide (organized chapter by chapter). We've included more questions for each chapter than you can productively consider in a single meeting—marching through all of them in a lockstep fashion is likely to result in mechanical and possibly superficial exploration of the questions and ideas they raise. Therefore, we think it's more beneficial for your group to select a subset of specific questions for discussion that are of particular interest to group members.

We want to emphasize that the purpose of the guiding questions is to provoke discussion, so they might lead the group into new areas not addressed by the original questions themselves. This is wonderful! The value of book study lies in helping move members along in their understanding of the book's content and connecting to questions and issues most salient to them.

If you decide to use the guiding questions to structure your study group meetings, we suggest that group members read over the questions before reading the chapter itself so they have a framework for thinking about the chapter's contents.

158

Book Study
Guide for
Examining
Mathematics
Practice
Through
Classroom
Artifacts

Structure 3: Combination of Structure 1 and 2

Of course, a third option is to combine the two structures. Select the format that best fits your group and the time frame you have set for studying the book.

Regardless of the structure you choose, we strongly recommend that each session concludes with a look forward to the next meeting. Take a few minutes before you end to identify, as a group, a purpose for reading the next chapter. You might decide to see how the next chapter addresses questions still outstanding for the group, to investigate implications for each person's own teaching, or to identify new ideas to consider.

Guiding Questions for Each Chapter

Chapter 1: Turning to the Evidence

1. What ideas from this chapter do you see yourself using in your classroom? Why? How?
2. Think back to when you were in elementary and/or middle school. What are your memories of mathematics? What instructional strategies did your teachers use? How effective do you feel they were?
3. In this chapter, the authors talk about the usefulness of artifacts. How do you think the study of artifacts will help you as a teacher? What questions do you have about using artifacts?
4. The authors recognize the pressure that high stakes tests bring. What ways do you balance the tension between test preparation and concept development in your own teaching?
5. In this chapter, the authors suggest that students may need to learn how to interpret mathematical models or representations and give the example of using base-10 blocks to teach place value in elementary mathematics. Discuss this example with your group.
6. The authors introduce the Skillful Use of Artifacts Framework as a way for teachers to focus attention on both the mathematical thinking and the mathematical content embodied in classroom artifacts. What do you think of this framework? How might it be useful to you as you analyze artifacts? What questions does it raise for you?
7. While you were reading the description of the upcoming chapters, which sounded the most intriguing? Why? What do you expect to learn there?
8. Generate a question this chapter caused you to wonder about. Bring it to the group for discussion.

Chapter 2: Describing and Interpreting Classroom Artifacts

1. What strategies from this chapter do you see yourself using? Why? How?
2. Generate a question this chapter caused you to wonder about. Bring it to the group for discussion.
3. Discuss Danny's work with your group. How is Danny thinking about addition? What evidence do you have for your interpretation of his understanding of addition?
4. Watch and discuss the *Kasage* video clip with your group. Describe Kasage's work. What does (and doesn't) Kasage seem to understand about multidigit addition? What's your evidence for your interpretations?

5. Watch and discuss the *Myrna* video clip with your group. Describe Myrna's work. What does Myrna understand and not understand about solving a division problem? What evidence supports your interpretation? How did the fact that Myrna is an English-language learner influence your interpretation?

6. Choose one of the problems from this chapter to use with a student in an interview like the interviews in the video clips. Make a copy of the Chapter 2 worksheet and fill in your description of the student's work and your interpretations and evidence. Bring in the student's work (and/or an audio or video clip of the interview) to share (and discuss) with your study group, adapting the study questions from the chapter to guide your discussion.

How was this process of working with material you had collected yourself similar to and/or different from the one you used to analyze the video clips that accompanied the chapter?

7. Choose a homework assignment (or a quiz or test) and give it to your whole class. Sort the papers into three piles: a "gets the idea" pile, a "somewhat gets it" pile, and a pile for students who seem to be really struggling (or whose solutions raise lots of questions for you). Which pile is the largest? Is it the pile that you expected? Compare with each other how you analyzed and sorted the work into piles. What was difficult about the task? Easy? What information did you learn about your class as a whole? What does this tell you about future instruction?

Chapter 3: Seeing the Potential in Student Thinking

1. What strategies from this chapter do you see yourself using? Why? How?

2. Generate a question this chapter caused you to wonder about. Bring it to the group for discussion.

3. Watch and discuss *Lemonade Lesson* video clip 1. Watch the video clip with an eye toward errors, partial understanding, or conceptual confusion as it emerges in the classroom discussion of the lemonade problem. Ask participants to say "stop" when they notice an error or misconception. Stop the video. Discuss the student's thinking and any insights about how the student's ideas relate to proportional reasoning. Resume the video until another error emerges and follow the same process. Continue the process until the group has watched the entire video clip. Discuss as a group all of the errors noticed, paying attention to both similarities and differences among the different

errors. What was the teacher's role in dealing with errors? What insights about teaching did this video give you?

4. Watch and discuss *Lemonade Lesson* video clip 2. Make copies of the blank Chapter 2 worksheets for each participant and use the same process outlined in question 3: watch the clip with an eye toward errors, partial understanding, or conceptual confusion as it emerges in the classroom discussion; have participants identify places in the video to stop and discuss the student's thinking; resume the video until someone identifies another error, partial understanding, or confusion. When you've finished the whole clip, discuss as a group everything you noticed, paying attention to both similarities and differences among the different errors. What was the teacher's role in dealing with errors? What insights about teaching did this video give you?

160

Book Study
Guide for
Examining
Mathematics
Practice
Through
Classroom
Artifacts

5. Think about a mathematical idea or topic you teach; what common errors do your students make? What could be the reasoning behind the errors? What are some ways you might use the errors to stimulate learning opportunities?

6. Bring copies of a piece of student work that shows an error that is typical or one that confuses you—make sure you have enough copies for the whole group. As a group, discuss what the nature of the error is, what the reasoning might be, and ways to use the error to stimulate learning opportunities.

7. Conduct diagnostic interviews with a few students to see how they are thinking about a problem. If possible, videotape the interviews. Bring in artifacts from an interview in which a student evidenced an error or misunderstanding. Discuss as a group what the error is, what the reasoning might be, and ways to use the error to stimulate learning opportunities.

Chapter 4: Keeping an Eye on Rigorous Mathematics

1. What strategies from this chapter do you see yourself using? Why? How?

2. Generate a question this chapter caused you to wonder about. Bring it to the group for discussion.

3. What mathematical frameworks or standards do you use in your school, district, and/or state to describe the key mathematical ideas and practices students need to learn?

4. In what ways does your school, district, and/or state support the development of mathematical practices as a goal of mathematics learning? What kinds of mathematical practices are students expected to display? How do you think this support (or lack of it) affects your teaching?

5. Bring in your textbook and analyze the way it treats big ideas. In small groups (perhaps grade-level groups or same-textbook groups), examine the textbooks using the following process:

   • Choose a unit to examine closely.
   • Read the unit introduction in the teachers' guide.
   • Review the chapter for the unit.
   • Complete the Chapter 4 worksheet *Examining your textbook.*

   • Reflect and discuss: How do the authors frame the unit/chapter from a mathematical perspective?
     a. What is the mathematical focus of the unit?
     b. How clearly is this focus articulated for the teacher? For the student?
     c. Is the primary emphasis on developing skills? Concepts? A combination?
     d. How do the authors connect skill development to underlying concepts?
     e. How do the authors emphasize the use of mathematical practices?

6. Analyze and discuss as a group the two lesson plans in the chapter.
   a. Extend the comparative analysis of Exercise 2. Compare and contrast the two lessons in terms of their connection to the Common Core State Standards. What mathematical practices are supported in these lessons? What mathematical content standards are the focus? Use examples to support your analysis.
   b. How might you change either of these lessons to increase the level of connection to the Common Core State Standards?

Chapter 5: Choosing, Using, and Connecting Representations

1. What strategies from this chapter do you see yourself using? Why? How?
2. Generate a question this chapter caused you to wonder about. Bring it to the group for discussion.
3. Discuss Larry's classroom scenario as it relates to the Common Core State Standards. What mathematical processes were used by students solving the Dots problem? What content standards were evident in the task?
4. Use the Dots problem with your students and bring back samples of their work to discuss. Use the Chapter 5 Worksheet to capture the methods/representations your students used. Did your students solve it in the same ways that Larry's students did? What methods did most students use? Were there any surprises? What did your students' methods and representations tell you about their understanding? What additional experiences might they need?
5. Discuss the Fraction Lesson video clip as it relates to the Common Core State Standards. What mathematical practices are students using? What mathematical content standards are the focus? What could be done additionally or differently to connect the content and the practices to the recommendations of the Common Core State Standards?
6. How do you choose, use, and connect representations in your math lessons? Choose a particular topic and discuss the following questions.
   a. What are some representations that you find are particularly useful?
   b. What are some ways that you would like to improve in your use of representations?
7. How has this chapter helped you think about representations? In what ways might it influence your practice?

Chapter 6: Putting It All Together

1. Generate a question this chapter caused you to wonder about. Bring it to the group for discussion.
2. This chapter introduced a new artifact as a tool for examining a lesson—a lesson graph. What was useful for you about a lesson graph for examining the mathematical story line of the lesson? What was not so useful?
3. Discuss the *Building Triangles* lesson in light of the Common Core State Standards. How does this lesson support mathematical practices? How does the content focus of the lesson relate to the recommendations of the Common Core Standards?
4. Discussing the *Multiplication* lesson, using the same process and questions that are outlined in question 3.
5. The authors end the book by stating that they wrote it to support teachers in using classroom artifacts to practice honing in on student thinking and errors, mathematical content and practices, and mathematical representations. What strategies from this book do you see yourself using? Why? How has this book helped you in using artifacts to deepen your practice? What do you see yourself continuing to explore?

Reading Reaction Sheet[2]

Facilitator/Recorder:

Group participants:

Date of reaction/discussion:

Chapter:

Question #1: What ideas and information from this chapter could be useful for classroom instruction?

Reactions:

Question #2:

Reactions:

Question #3:

Reactions:

Question #4:

Reactions:

---

[2]Adapted from Cunningham and Cunningham (2010).

Index